CARMARTHEN TO FISHGUARD

Vic Mitchell and Keith Smith

MP Middleton Press

Front cover: Carmarthen engine shed is in the background, as no. 5054 Earl of Ducie *reversed onto an up train in June 1963. (N.K.Harrop/Bentley coll.)*

Back cover: No. 47582 waits to leave Carmarthen with the 11.34 to Milford Haven on 10th January 1989. The logo was probably the largest ever seen on a British locomotive. (H.Ballantyne)

Published January 2010

ISBN 978 1 906008 66 6

Design Deborah Esher

Published by
Middleton Press
Easebourne Lane
Midhurst
West Sussex
GU29 9AZ
Tel: 01730 813169
Fax: 01730 812601
Email: info@middletonpress.co.uk
www.middletonpress.co.uk

Printed in the United Kingdom by Henry Ling Limited, at the Dorset Press, Dorchester, DT1 1HD

CONTENTS

INDEX

ACKNOWLEDGEMENTS

We are very grateful for the assistance received from many of those mentioned in the credits also to A.R.Carder, L.Crosier, G.Croughton, S.C.Jenkins, M.A.N.Johnston, J.Langford, N.Langridge, B.Lewis, D.T.Rowe, Mr D. and Dr S.Salter and especially, our always supportive wives, Barbara Mitchell and Janet Smith.

I. Route map for the 1960s. The Cardigan line closed on 10th September 1962 and the Neyland branch followed on 15th June 1964.

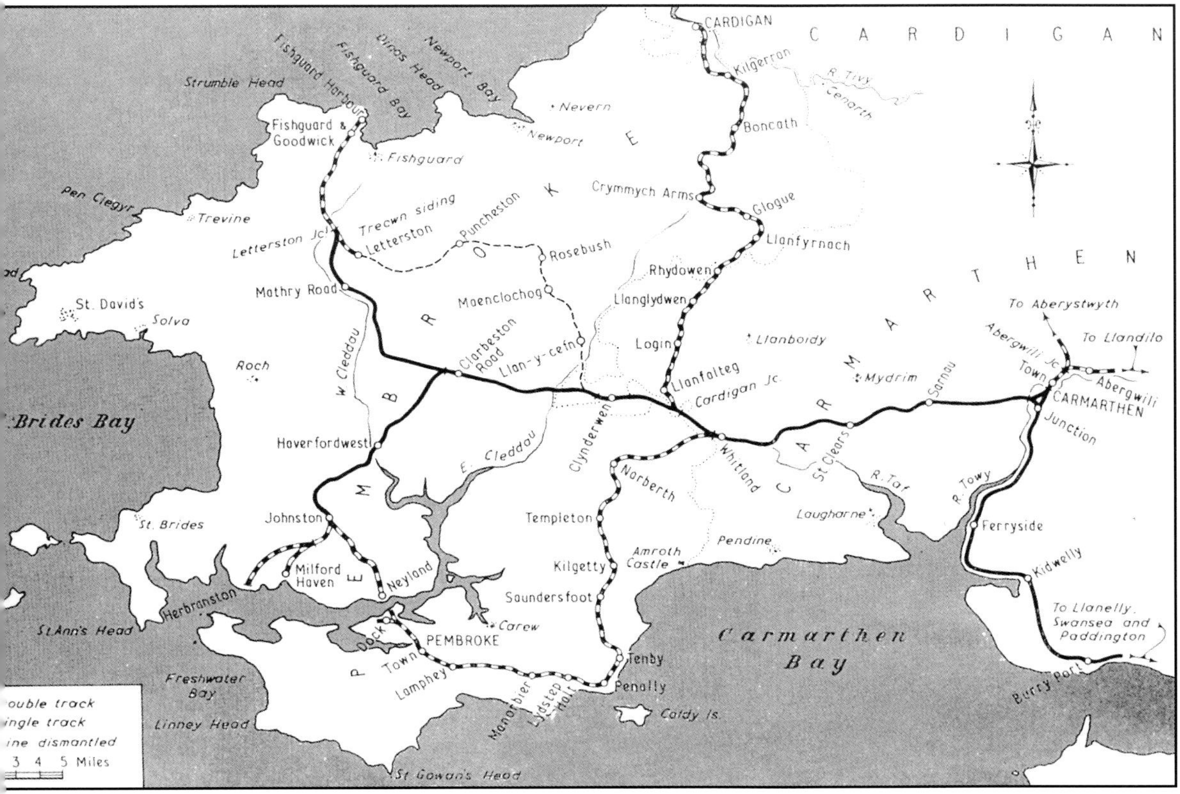

GEOGRAPHICAL SETTING

Carmarthen is situated near the tidal limit of the River Towy and was the county town. The line climbs for two miles out of the valley and dips to cross the Afon Cynlin north of St. Clears. It runs close to the Avon Taf in the vicinity of Whitland.

Thereafter it climbs at around 1 in 100 to Clynderwen, where it passes over the watershed into the valley of the Eastern Cleddau, which is south flowing. There is a further climb to Clarbeston Road, from where the Milford Haven branch descends to the substantial town of Haverfordwest.

The area is composed of ancient sedimentary rocks, but on the final 15 miles of the journey to Fishguard there are a number of small bands of hard intrusive rock, which often stand out in the landscape.

The final few miles are on a steep descent to the well sheltered waters around Fishguard Harbour, which is east facing and thus sheltered from the prevailing winds.

The first 15 miles of the route were built in Carmarthenshire and most of the remainder of it, including the branches, were in Pembrokeshire.

The maps are to the scale of 25ins to 1 mile, with north at the top, unless otherwise indicated. Furthermore, Welsh spelling and hyphenation has varied over the years and so we have generally used the most recent form, as have the railways.

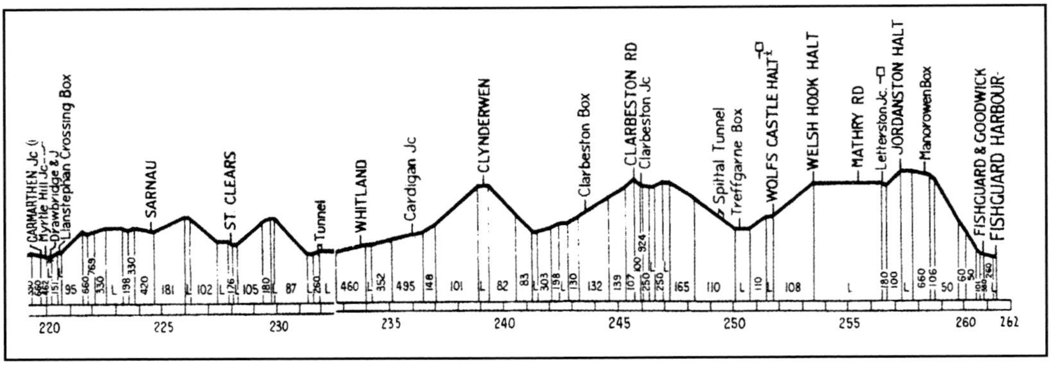

HISTORICAL BACKGROUND

The South Wales Railway reached a station south of Carmarthen from Swansea in 1852. The company extended its operation to Haverfordwest on 2nd January 1854. A further extension to "Milford Haven" followed on 15th April 1856, although the station was in Neyland. All these lines were built to the broad gauge of 7ft 0¼ins, became part of the Great Western Railway in 1862 and were converted to standard gauge in May 1872.

A branch to Carmarthen Town opened on 1st March 1860. It ran north to Conwil and was part of the Carmarthen & Cardigan Railway until 1881. A line from Llandeilo joined it in 1864.

Trains ran north to Cardigan from Whitland from 1886. However, the southern part of the branch to Llanfrynach had received freight from 1873.

The Milford Railway from Johnston to Milford Haven opened on 7th September 1863 and became part of the GWR in 1896. It was broad gauge until 1872.

Map I shows a line of dashes, which formed part of the first route to Fishguard. Narberth Road & Maenclochog and Rosebush & Fishguard were separate companies. Traffic began on their routes on 19th September 1876, but a two-hour road connection was provided to Fishguard from Rosebush. The North Pembrokeshire & Fishguard Railway completed the route to Letterston on 11th April 1895. There were several periods of closure until the GWR took over in 1898. It extended the line to Fishguard (town) on 1st July 1899 and to Fishguard Harbour on 30th August 1906. This was also the date of the opening of its direct route from Clarbeston Road to Letterston Junction. The old route closed to passengers on 25th October 1937 and as no photographs of it are available, we simply include it on the maps. Most of the line west of Puncheston closed on 3rd November 1942 and east thereof on 16th May 1949; Letterston was served until 1st March 1965.

The branch from Johnston to Neyland closed to passengers on 15th June 1964, but the other routes remain open.

The GWR lasted until nationalisation in 1948, when its routes became part of the Western Region of British Railways. Privatisation in 1996 resulted in South Wales & West providing services ("South" was dropped in 1998). However, after reorganisation in 2001, Wales & Borders became the franchisee. Arriva Trains Wales took over in December 2003.

London services were provided by Great Western Trains from 4th February 1996, this changing to First Great Western on 1st April 2006.

Station closures and freight withdrawals are given in the captions.

PASSENGER SERVICES

Owing to the confusing change of names, the final versions will be used throughout this section. The figures in brackets refer to Sunday trains, in the Summer; the Winter service was usually sparse.

Fishguard

The initial service was provided by road with a horse-drawn coach from Rosebush, weekdays only. After the route was completed via that place, there were generally only two or three trains each weekday. Completion of the direct route brought four or five local trains from Clynderwen, plus boat trains, usually two.

Local trains increased steadily, reaching nine in the late 1940s, but they declined and were withdrawn completely in 1964, leaving only the two daily boat trains, in most periods.

Milford Haven

Most timetables in the 19th century offered five arrivals, weekdays only. During the next century the figures were 9 to 12 (1 to 3). In 2009, they were 11 (7).

Neyland

The 19th century figures were mostly 7 (2) and the 20th century ones were 11 to 13 (2 or 3). The final full year (1963) offered seven (3). Two of these ran from Paddington, daily.

Sleeping cars were provided to all three destinations for most of the steam era and to the first two until May 1984.

Traffic Supt., J. Phillips.] **MAENCLOCHOG.** [Gen. Man., J. B. Macaulay.

Mls										
	Clynderwen..dep	7 45	1120	3 0	8 0	**Fishguard** (per Coach)	gov	8 15	aft	gov
1¾	Baeg (F. S.)......	**a**	**a**	....	**a**	**Rosebush** (Train)..dep	6 30	1020	1 0	6 45
3¾	Llanycefn........	8 2	1137	3 15	8 17	Maenclochog	6 40	1027	1 10	6 55
6¼	Maenclochog	8 19	1153	3 30	8 33	Llanycefn............	6 56	1040	1 26	7 11
8	**Rosebush** ....arr	8 25	12 0	3 35	8 40	Baeg (F. S.)..........	**a**	...	**a**	**a**
18	**Fishguard** (Ch) ,,	....	....	5 30	....	**Clynderwen 29,28**arr	7 10	1155	1 40	7 25

a Stop when required.

July 1878

CLYNDERWEN and FISHGUARD HARBOUR (1st and 3rd class). Great Western.

Miles	**Down.**	Week Days.												
		mrn	mrn	mrn	mrn	**m**	**m**	**m**	**m**	aft	**m**	aft	aft	aft
	Clynderwen..........dep.	....	....	9 45	1045	1213	....	....	....	2 40	5 55	6 10	8 10	1031
6½	Clarbeston Road..........	....	....	9 57	....	1227	....	....	....	....	6 10	....	8 20	....
3¾	Llanycefn	....	....	....	1055	....			....	2 50	....	6 20	....	....
6¾	Maenclochog	....	....	....	11 6	....			....	3 1	....	6 31	....	....
8¼	Rosebush	....	....	....	1114	....			....	3 9	....	6 39	....	....
12¼	Puncheston	....	....	....	1127	....			....	3 22	....	6 52	....	....
17¼	Letterston..........	....	....	....	1140	....			....	3 35	....	7 5	....	....
23¼	Fishguard and Goodwick ...	7 30	8 55	1030	12 0	1 3	2 0	2 40	3 45	4 1	6 46	7 28	8 50	1112
24	**Fishguard Harbour**....arr.	7 32	8 57	1035	....	1 5	2 2	2 42	3 47	4 5	6 48	7 30	8 55	1115

March 1909

May 1889

Great Western Railway.

EXPRESS SERVICES BETWEEN ENGLAND AND THE

SOUTH OF IRELAND, via MILFORD HAVEN.

To and from Waterford.

The Steamers leave New Milford daily (except Mondays) immediately after the arrival of the 5 45 aft. Express Train from Paddington, due at 1 45 mrn. A Steamer also leaves New Milford for Waterford on Mondays, at 7 mrn. after arrival of the 9 15 aft. Train from Paddington, due at 6 50 mrn.

The Steamers leave Waterford, Adelphi Wharf, at 5 aft. (Irish Time) each week day, after arrival of Trains from Limerick, &c. **The Train from New Milford waits the arrival of the boat in all cases.** Fifteen minutes allowed at Gloucester by the Boat Train for Breakfast.

On Sundays a Steamer leaves Waterford, North Wharf, at 7 a.m., in connection with the 5 p.m. Train from New Milford due in London at 2 15 a.m. Passengers for this Steamer holding through Tickets from Stations beyond Waterford may sleep on board on Saturday nights, but they are not allowed to go on board before 9 p.m.

Under no circumstances are Third Class Passengers allowed the use of the Saloons.

To and from Cork.

The Steamers leave New Milford every Tuesday, Thursday, and Saturday, at 8 aft. on arrival of the 10 20 mrn. Express Train from Paddington, and are due to reach Passage at about 8 mrn. on the following mornings. They proceed from Passage to Cork as soon as the tide serves. Trains also leave Passage for Cork at frequent intervals.

From Cork (Albert or Penrose Quays) and the City of Cork Steam Company's Wharf, Passage, every Monday, Wednesday, and Friday, as per Table below, in connection with the 2 45 mrn. or 8 40 mrn. Fast Trains from New Milford to London and all parts of England.

Third Class Passengers are also booked between Great Western Railway and Ireland by Through Trains as below:—

THROUGH TIME TABLE—WEEK DAYS.

To IRELAND.		To Cork calling at Passage.	To Cork.	To Waterford.
London (Paddington)	dep	10 20 mrn		5 45 aft
Portsmouth	"	8 0 —		2 15 —
Southampton	"	8 50 —		3 37 —
Dover (L. C. & D.)	"	4 § 0 —		12 0 —
Reading	"	11 20 —		5 51 —
Oxford	"	9 25 —		5 47 —
Swindon	"	12 30 aft		7 32 —
Cheltenham	"	12 40 —		8 10 —
Gloucester	"	1 10 —		8 45 —
Plymouth, *via* Bristol	"	8†35 mrn		2 30 —
Exeter ditto	"	10†30 —		4 55 —
Bristol, *v.* Severn Tunnl	"	1 18 aft		7 50 —
Birmingham (Snw Hll)	"	10 0 mrn		4 30 —
Worcestr (Shrub H.) *via*	"	11‡17 —		6 15 —
Shrewsbury do. (Nport	"	10 35 —		5 55 —
Hereford ditto	"	12 35 aft		7 50 —
Newport	"	2 42 —		9 48 —
Cardiff	"	3 5 —		10 10 —
Swansea	"	4 20 —		11 15 —
New Milford	arr	6 55 —		1 45 mrn
New Milford (Steamer)	dep	....	....	2 0 mrn
Waterford	arr	....	mrn	10 15 —
Waterford	dep	....	1015	1 20 aft
Carrick-on-Suir	arr	....	1041	1 46 —
Clonmel	"	....	1111	2 16 —
Fethard	"	....	12 5	4 32 —
Caher	"	....	1133	2 38 —
Tipperary	"	....	1158	3 2 —
Limerick Junction	"	....	1210	3 20 —
Limerick	"	....	1 15	4 30 —
Ennis	"	....	....	6 4 —
Listowel	"	....	....	7 50 —
Tralee (W. & L.)	"	....	....	9 0 —
Mallow Junction	"	....	1 25	7 15 —
Killarney	"	....	3 18	9 32 —
Tralee (G. S. & W.)	"	....	4 9	10 25 —
Cork *	"	....	2 15	8 10 —
Waterford	dep	....	....	2 30 aft
Kilkenny	arr	....	....	3 37 —
Maryborough	"	....	....	4 45 —
Mountmellick	"	....	....	5 20 —
Waterford	dep	....	....	3 30 aft
Dungarvan	arr	....	....	4 50 —
Lismore	"	....	....	5 30 —
New Milford (for Cork)	dep	8 0 aft	....	....
Passage	arr	8 0 mrn	....	....
Cork	"	According to Tide.		

IRISH TIME (Waterford to Lismore).

‡ Foregate Street. § 1&2 class.

† 1st and 2nd class only; 3rd class passengers must leave Plymouth at 6 45 and Exeter at 9 35 a.m.

c Not on Mondays from New Milford to Cardiff.

From IRELAND. Cork dep / Passage " / New Milford (frm Cork) arr		From Wtrfd	Frm Cork calling at Passage. See side.	SUNDAYS.
		mrn		mrn
Lismore	dep	11 50		....
Dungarvan	"	1 30		....
Waterford	arr	3 15		....
Mountmellick	dep	9 20		....
Maryborough	"	10 50		....
Kilkenny	"	12 40		....
Waterford	arr	2 20		....
Cork	dep	6 0		....
Tralee (G. S. & W.)	"	6 0		
Killarney	"	6 52		
Mallow Junction	"	7 0		
Tralee (W. & L.)	"	6 0		
Listowel	"	6 55		
Ennis	"	8 18		
Limerick	"	11 20		
Limerick Junction	"	12 25		
Tipperary	"	12 43		
Caher	"	1 18		
Fethard	"	10 55		
Clonmel	"	1 48		
Carrick-on-Suir	"	2 29		
Waterford	arr	3 10		
Waterford (Steamr)	dep	5 0		
		mrn		
New Milfrd (fm Waterfrd)	a	1 30	mrn	mrn
New Milford	dep	2c45	8 40	3 55
Swansea	arr	4c55	11 25	6 15
Cardiff	"	5c53	12 39	7 30
Newport	"	6 17	1 3	8 5
Hereford, *via* Newport	"	9 10	3 33	1015
Shrewsbury ditto	"	11 10	5 30	1240
Worcester (Shrub H) do.	"	11 13	5‡0	1155
Birmingham (Snow H.	"	12 26	6 15	8 13
Bristol, *v.* Severn Tunnl	"	8 18	2 15	1045
Exeter ditto	"	11 43	4*b*0	6 30
Plymouth ditto	"	2 20	5*b*55	9 28
Gloucester	"	7 30	2 27	5 22
Cheltenham	"	8 25	3 10	5 50
Swindon (for Refresh-	ar	8 50	3 10	3 25
ments)	dp	9 0	3 20	3 35
Oxford	arr	10 55	5 30	5 22
Reading	"	9 53	4 13	5 29
Dover (L. C. & D.)	"	4 58	9§54	12 4
Southampton	"	12*e*0	7 2	8 12
Portsmouth	"	12*e*51	7 48	9 0
London (Paddington)	"	10 45	5 15	7 20

IRISH TIME (Lismore to Waterford).

e Via Bristol and Salisbury.

¶ Passengers by this train travel *via* Bristol to London, Plymouth, and places beyond Bristol.

* Passengers to Cork, *via* Waterford, can only book through to and from Limerick Junction.

b 1st and 2nd class only; 3rd class Passengers arrive at Exeter at 5 37, and Plymouth at 7 30 aft.

CORK SAILINGS FOR MAY, 1889.

Passenger, General Cargo, and Cattle Boats. [* Irish Time.

Date.			From Cork. Irish Time.	From Passage.*	Date.			From Cork. Irish Time.	From Passage.*
Wednesday,	May	1....	6 0 aft	Direct	Friday,	May	17..	6 0 aft	Direct
Friday,	"	3....	6 0 —	Direct	Monday,	"	20..	6 0 —	Direct
Monday,	"	6....	6 0 —	Direct	Wednesday,	"	22..	6 30 —	Direct
Wednesday,	"	8....	6 0 —	Direct	Friday,	"	24..	3 0 —	5 30 aft
Friday,	"	10....	3 0 —	5 30 aft	Monday,	"	27..	5 30 —	Direct
Monday,	"	13....	5 30 —	Direct	Wednesday,	"	29..	6 0 —	Direct
Wednesday,	"	15....	6 0 —	Direct	Friday,	"	31..	6 0 —	Direct

For further information see the Company's Time Books and Special Bills; or apply to Mr. E. Fogg, Railway Terminus, Limerick; Mr. W. D. M'Namara, G.W.R., Adelphi Wharf, Waterford; Mr. Stanton, Patrick's Quay, Cork; the Cork Steamship Company Limited, Cork; the Station Master's or Marine Superintendent's Offices, New Milford; or the Company's District Agent, Adelphi Wharf, Waterford; also at any of the Company's Stations.

Paddington Terminus, May, 1889. **HY. LAMBERT, General Manager.**

July 1929

CLYNDERWEN and FISHGUARD HARBOUR (Rail Motor Cars—One class only).

Miles	Down.	Week Days only.		
		mrn	aft	aft
	Clynderwen dep.	1045	2 55	6 5
3¼	Llanycefn	1056	3 7	6 16
6¼	Maenclochog	11 7	3 22	6 27
8¼	Rosebush	1113	3 31	6 33
12¼	Puncheston	1125	3 46	6 45
13¾	Castlebythe Halt	1128	3 49	6 48
15¼	Beulah Halt	1134	3 55	6 54
17¼	Letterston	1138	4 2	6 58
20	Jordanston Halt	1146	4 10	7 6
23¼	**Fishguard & Goodwick**	1153	4 17	7 13
23¾	**Fishguard Harbour** arr.	1155		

Miles	Up.	Week Days only.	
		mrn	aft
	Fishguard Harbour dep.		
½	**Fishguard & Goodwick**	9 10	4 35
3¾	Jordanston Halt	9 20	4 45
6½	Letterston	9 28	4 54
8½	Beulah Halt	9 33	4 58
10¼	Castlebythe Halt	9 39	5 4
11¼	Puncheston	9 42	5 7
15¼	Rosebush	9 54	5 19
17	Maenclochog	10 0	5 25
20	Llanycefn	1010	5 35
23¼	**Clynderwen** 67 arr.	1020	5 45

June 1869

Swindon, Gloucester, Chepstow, Newport, Cardiff, Neath, Swansea, Llanelly, Carmarthen, and New Milford (for Milford Haven).—Great Western. | Eng., W. G. Owen.

Miles from London.	Down.			Week Days. mrn	mrn	a	mrn	1,2,3	mrn	aft	aft	aft	aft	exp	aft	aft	Sundays. mrn	mrn	mrn	aft	aft	aft
	Paddington Sta., London 8 ..dep			....	....	6 0	9 15	1010	1145	2 0	....	4 50	5 [illegible]	6 30	8 10	9 0		....	10 0	2 30	8 10	9 0
	8 ,, (Victoria) ,,			....	....	....	....	6 28	8 30	....	....	3 27	3 27	....	6 31	b		....	8 30	1 30	....	b
	8 ,, (Knsngtn ,,			....	....	....	....	6 48	8 52	....	....	3 49	3 49	....	6 50	....		....	8 52	1 52	....	....
	Reading 8 .. ,,			....	....	7 5	9 35	8 35	1130	3 0	....	5 15	6 33	7 12	9 20	....		....	1136	3 57	9 20	....
	Oxford 21&8 ,,			..	....	7c15	9 20	....	1135	2 25	....	5 35	6 3	....	9 10	....		..	7e40	4 10	8 30	....
	Didcot 8 .... ,,			....	....	7 43	1025	9 30	1210	3 37	....	6 15	7 45	7 45	9 55	....		....	1223	4 40	9 55	....
	Fm Weymouth, Dorchestr, &c., pp. 7 & 10			1,2,3	1,2,3	1&2	1&2	\	1,2,3	1&2	1,2,3	1&2	1&2	exp	1&2	1 cl.		1,2,3	1,2,3	1&2	1&2	1 cl
				mrn	mrn	mrn	exp		aft	aft	aft	aft	aft	aft	aft	aft		mrn	aft	aft	aft	aft
77¼	Swindon June. dep			....	8 10	9 12	1115	....	1 40	4 30	....	7 2	8 50	8 50	1120	....		....	1 45	5 41	1120	....
81¼	Purton			....	8 20	....	....	....	1 50	4 41	....	....	9 0	9 0	....	....		....	1 55	5 50	....	....
85½	Minety			....	8 30	9 23	....	....	2 2	4 51	....	....	9 10	9 10	....	....		....	2 5	6 0	....	....
95½	Cirencester dep			....	8 20	9 25	1120	....	2 0	4 45	....	7 5	....	....	....	....		....	1 55	5 55	....	....
	Cirencester arr			....	9 5	10 5	1155	....	2 40	5 20	....	7 50	....	....	....	....		....	2 55	6 25	....	....
91½	Tetbury Road			....	8 47	9 47	....	....	2 23	5 8	....	....	9 25	9 25	1148	....		....	2 20	6 15	1148	....
99¾	Brimscomb, near			....	9 5	10 4	....	....	2 43	5 28	....	....	9 43	9 43	....	....		....	2 40	6 35	....	....
102½	Stroud 1 [Chalford			....	9 15	1014	1210	....	2 53	5 38	....	7 47	9 53	9 53	12 8	12 8		....	2 50	6 42	12 8	12 8
105	Stonehouse			....	9 24	1022	....	....	3 3	5 47	....	....	10 2	10 2	....	....		....	3 0	6 50	....	....
114	Glo'ster 21, 169 ar			....	9 42	1040	1225	....	3 23	6 5	....	8 10	1020	1020	1235	1235		..	3 20	7 10	1235	1235
120	Cheltenhm (St. d			6 10	....	1025	1155	....	3 0	....	6 0	7 45	....	....	1215	....		7 45	[illegible]	..	1215	
	James's Sq.) 170 a			....	10 5	1130	1250	....	3 45	6 25	....	8 38	1040	1040	1 5	1 5		....	3 [illegible]	7 30	....	
	Fm Birmingham 168			1,2,3	—	1,2,3	exp	....	1,2,3	—	1,2,3	exp			1&2			1,2,3	1,2,3	—	1&2	
—	Gloucester ......dep			6 35	Stop	1110	1230	....	3 30	Stop	7 0	8 15	....		1250			8 15	3 30	Stop	1250	
121½	Grange Court 21 ..			6 50	....	1126	....	....	3 47	....	7 16	....	....		....			8 30	3 48	....	....	
144½	Hereford 21 arr			....	....	12 5	1 45	....	5 0	....	....	....	....		....			....	5 5	....	....	
125	Newnham			7 0	....	1135	....	....	4 0	....	7 25	....	....		1 12			8 40	3 58	....	1 12	
130½	Awre (for Blakeney)			7 8	....	1143	....	....	4 8	....	7 33	....	....		....			8 48	4 6	....	....	
133¾	Lydney			7 22	1,2,3	1156	1 2	....	4 18	1,2,3	7 46	....	....		1 31			9 0	4 18	1,2,3	1 31	
136½	Woolaston ..[Abbey)			7 31	mrn	12 4	....	....	4 26	aft	7 54	....	....		....			9 8	4 26	aft	....	
141½	Chepstow (Tintern			7 44	1115	1216	1 17	....	4 40	6 5	8 5	8 55	....		1 49			9 18	4 39	8 5	1 49	
145½	Portskewet Jn. 16 ar			7 54	1125	1225	1 27	....	4 50	6 15	9 15	....	....		....			9 27	4 47	8 15	....	
—	16 Bristl Templ St. d			6 15	10 0	10 0	1215	....	3 10	5 0	6 50	....	....		....			8 10	3 9	7 20	....	
—	Portskewet Jn. dep			8 2	1135	1227	1 32	....	4 55	6 20	8 20	....	....		....			9 35	4 49	8 31	....	
151½	Magor			8 13	....	1235	....	....	....	6 31	....	....	....		....			9 47	5 1	8 43	....	
155	Llanwern	1,2,3		8 21	....	1247	....	....	....	6 39	....	....	....		....			9 56	5 9	8 51	....	
158¾	Newport 27, a	mrn		8 30	1155	1255	1 52	....	5 20	6 47	8 40	9 25	....		2 18			10 3	5 20	9 0	2 18	
	30, 131, 136 d	7 0		8 35	12 0	1 0	2 0	....	5 25	6 50	8 45	9 30			2 21			1010	5 25	9 5	2 21	
164	Marshfield	7 12		....	....	1 12	....	....	5 37	7 2	....	....			....			1022	5 36	9 17	....	
170½	Cardiff 31 arr	7 26		8 55	1220	1 25	2 20	....	5 55	7 15	9 5	9 50			2 43			1036	5 47	9 30	2 41	
	Cardiff 31 dep	7 30		9 0	—	1 30	2 25	....	6 0			9 55			2 45			1039	5 49	....	2 45	
172¾	Ely, fr Llandaff	7 35		....	Stop	1 35	....	....	6 7			....			....			1046	5 54	....	....	
174½	St. Fagans	7 42		....	....	1 42	....	....	6 14			....			....			1053	5 59	....	....	
177¼	Peterston	7 50		....	....	1 50	....	....	6 22			....			....			11 0	6 5	....	....	
181½	Llantrssant 31	8 2		9 22	....	2 3	....	....	6 35			....			....			1110	6 15	....	....	
186¾	Pencoed	8 15		....	....	2 16	....	....	6 51			....			....			1121	6 33	....	....	
190½	Bridgend 29 ..	8 25		9 42	....	2 26	3 58	....	7 3			1020			3 20			1131	6 43	....	3 20	
196¼	Pyle 29	8 40		....	....	2 40	....	....	7 18			....			....			1145	6 58	....	....	
202¾	Port Talbot ..	8 54		1010	....	2 54	3 20	....	7 33			1051			3 44			12 0	7 15	....	3 44	
206	Briton Ferry ..	9 2		....	....	3 4	....	....	7 42			....			....			12 8	7 25	....	....	
208¾	Neath 30	9 10		1024	....	3 13	3 32	....	7 52			11 3			3 57			1216	7 38	....	3 57	
211½	Llansamlet 30	9 19	1,2,3	....	1,2,3	3 22	....	....	8 3			1112			....		1,2,3	1225	7 49	....	....	
214¾	Landore ....[2 1	9 27	mrn	1039	aft	3 30	3 47	....	8 10			1119			4 16		mrn	1235	8 0	....	4 16	
21 ½	Swnsea 127, d	....	7 45	1030	1230	3 15	3 45	....	8 0			1112			4 5		9 15	....	7 55	....	4 5	
	30 (High St.) a	9 35	....	1048	....	3 45	4 5	....	8 20			1130			4 30		....	1240	8 10	....	4 30	
—	Landore		7 55	1045	1240	3 35	3 52	....	8 15			1123	....		4 21		9 25	—	8 7	....	4 21	
219½	Gower Road 127 ..		8 10	11 0	1255	3 50	....	....	8 29			....	....		....		9 37	Stop	8 19	....	....	
221½	Loughor		8 16	11 6	1 1	3 56	....	....	8 34			....	....		....		9 42	....	8 24	....	....	
224¾	Llanelly 127		8 25	1115	1 10	4 5	4 18	....	8 45			1146	....		4 46		9 51	....	8 33	....	4 46	
229¾	Pembrey (Burry Pt.)		8 35	1125	1 20	4 15	4 28	....	8 55			....	....		....		10 0	....	8 43	....	....	
234¼	Kidwelly		8 45	1137	1 30	4 27	n	....	9 6			....	....		5 4		1011	....	8 52	....	5 4	
238½	Ferryside		8 56	1151	1 39	4 39	4 50	....	9 18			....	....		....		1024	....	9 4	....	....	
245	Carmarthen Junc..		9 8	12 4	1 50	4 52	5 3	....	9 30			1217	....		5 23		1040	....	9 15	....	5 23	
—	Carmarthen dp		8 35	....	—	....	....		....			....	....		....		—	....	....		....	
	For Cardigan. 31 ar		9 15	1215	Stop	5 10	5 10		9 37			....	....		5 30		Stop	....	....		....	
253½	St. Clears		9 26	1227	....	5 23	5 23		....	....		1234	....		....		....	....	9 36		....	
258¾	Whitland 31		9 40	1243	....	5 36	5 36		....	....		1245	....		5 50		....	....	9 52		5 50	
264½	Narberth Road		9 53	1257	....	5 48	5 48		....	....		....	....		d		....	....	10 7		d	
270½	Clarbeston Road ..		10 7	1 11	....	6 2	6 2		....	....		....	....		....		....	....	1023		....	
276	Haverfordwst	1,2,3	1019	1 22	1&2	6 13	6 13		....	....		1 20	....		6 26		1,2,3	1,2,3	1034		6 26	
280¾	Johnston	mrn	1033	1 36	aft	6 23	6 28		....	....		....	....		6 41		mrn	aft	1050		6 41	
—	Johnston dep	9 10	1120	1 40	5 20	6 38	6 38		....	....		....	....		....		1120	5 20	....		....	
—	Milford ..arr	9 20	1135	1 55	5 35	6 53	6 53		....	....		....	....		....		1130	5 35	....		....	
285½	New Milford 2 arr		1045	1 50	....	6 42	6 42		....	....		1 40	....		6 50		....	....	11 5		6 50	

c 1,2,3 class from Oxford to Gloucester and Cheltenham and the South Wales Line.

e 3rd class from Oxford to Gloucester and Cheltenham.

d Stops on Sunday mornings only.

1 3rd class to Stations East and West of Portskewet.

1, Station for Nailsworth and Wooton-under-Edge. 2, for Milford Haven and Ireland.

1,2,3 class.

n Stops when required to set down pass. from London, Birmingham, Gloucester, or Newport and intermediate Stas., on giving notice to the Guard at Llanelly.

b Limited Mail.—A limited number of 1st class Passengers booked from London only, at Express Fares, to Stations shown, and places should be secured beforehand.

a 3rd class to Stations on the South Wales Line and to Ireland; also from London and Reading to Gloucester and Cheltenham.

July 1949

CLARBESTON ROAD and FISHGUARD HARBOUR—(Third class only)

Miles		Week Days a.m A	a.m		p.m	p.m	p.m	p.m		p.m	p.m	1st and 3rd class	p.m L		Suns. p.m	
	Clarbeston Road... dep	9 50	111[illegible]	..	1250	4 20	5 5	6 50	..	7 30	9 10		10 8	..	9 10	..
6	Wolf's Castle Halt......	10 2	112[illegible]	..	1 2	4 32	5 17	..	..	7 42	9 22		..	..	9 22	..
7¾	Welsh Hook Halt.......	10 6	113[illegible]	..	1 6	4 36	5 21	..	..	7 46	9 26		..	..	9 26	..
9¾	Mathry Road...........	1011	1136	..	1 11	4 41	5 26	7 5	..	7 51	9 31		..	..	9 31	..
11¾	Jordanston Halt........	1016	1141	..	1 16	4 46	5 31	..	..	7 56	9 36		..	..	9 36	..
15	Fishguard and Goodwick	1023	1148	..	1 23	4 53	5 38	7 19	..	8 3	9 43		..	..	9 43	..
15½	Fishguard Harbour arr	1026	1151	..	1 26	4 56	5 41	7 22	..	8 6	9 46		1035	..	9 46	..

Miles		Week Days a.m N		a.m	non		p.m	p.m	p.m	p.m		p.m			Suns. p.m	
	Fishguard Harbour dep	7 35	..	1020	12 0	..	2 15	4 10	5 50	6 40	..	8 15	..	..	6 15	..
½	Fishguard and Goodwick	7 38	..	1023	12 3	..	2 18	4 15	5 53	6 43	..	8 18	..	..	6 18	..
3¾	Jordanston Halt........	7 48	..	1033	1213	..	2 28	4 25	6 3	6 53	..	8 28	..	..	6 28	..
5¾	Mathry Road...........	7 53	..	1038	1218	..	2 34	4 31	6 9	6 58	..	8 33	..	..	6 33	..
7¾	Welsh Hook Halt.......	7 57	..	1042	1222	..	2 38	4 35	6 13	7 2	..	8 37	..	..	6 37	..
9½	Wolf's Castle Halt......	8 2	..	1047	1227	..	2 43	4 40	6 18	7 7	..	8 42	..	..	6 42	..
15½	Clarbeston Road ....arr	8 13	..	1058	1238	..	2 54	4 51	6 29	7 18	..	8 53	..	..	6 53	..

A Dep. Neyland 9 0 a.m. (Table 104)

L Through Restaurant Car Train from London (Paddington) dep. 3 55 p.m. (Table 104)

N To Neyland arr. 8 47 a.m. (Table 104)

1. Carmarthen to Fishguard

CARMARTHEN

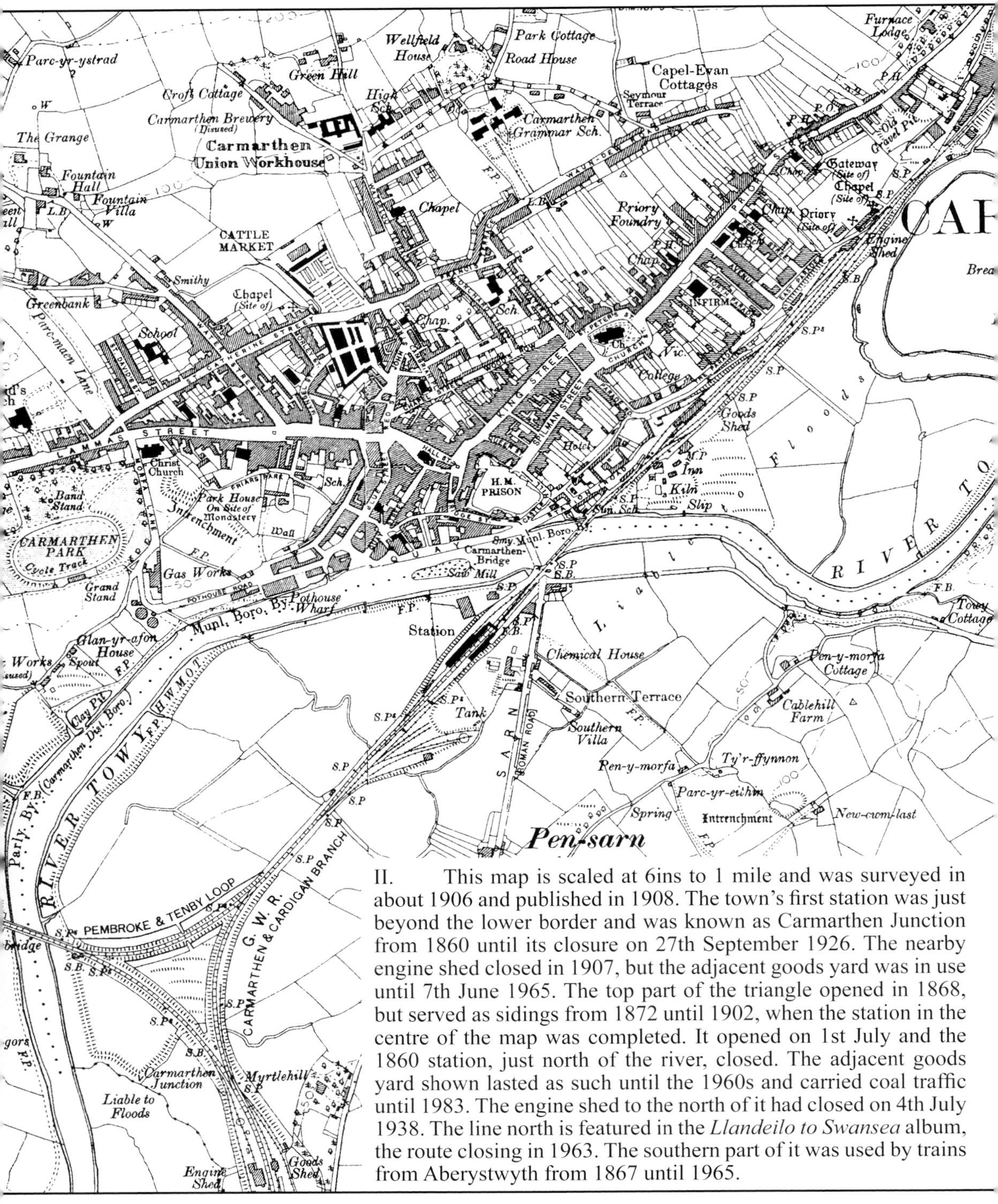

II. This map is scaled at 6ins to 1 mile and was surveyed in about 1906 and published in 1908. The town's first station was just beyond the lower border and was known as Carmarthen Junction from 1860 until its closure on 27th September 1926. The nearby engine shed closed in 1907, but the adjacent goods yard was in use until 7th June 1965. The top part of the triangle opened in 1868, but served as sidings from 1872 until 1902, when the station in the centre of the map was completed. It opened on 1st July and the 1860 station, just north of the river, closed. The adjacent goods yard shown lasted as such until the 1960s and carried coal traffic until 1983. The engine shed to the north of it had closed on 4th July 1938. The line north is featured in the *Llandeilo to Swansea* album, the route closing in 1963. The southern part of it was used by trains from Aberystwyth from 1867 until 1965.

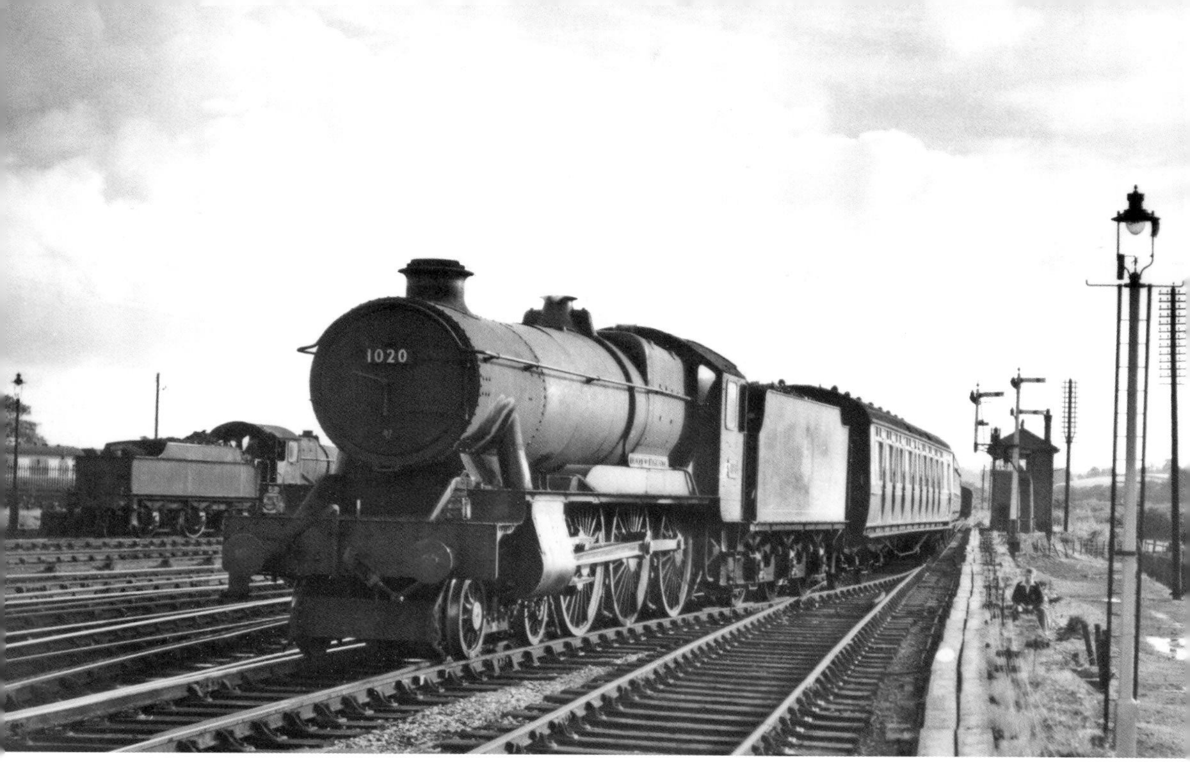

1. Approaching platform 3 from the south in August 1952 is no. 1020 *County of Monmouth* with a train from Swansea. On the right is South Box, which was in use from 1902 until 7th August 1972. (M.Whitehouse coll.)

2. A northward panorama from July 1958 has the fitting shed on the right, then a line of milk tankers with the three through platforms in the centre. On the left is a short parcels platform. (H.C.Casserley)

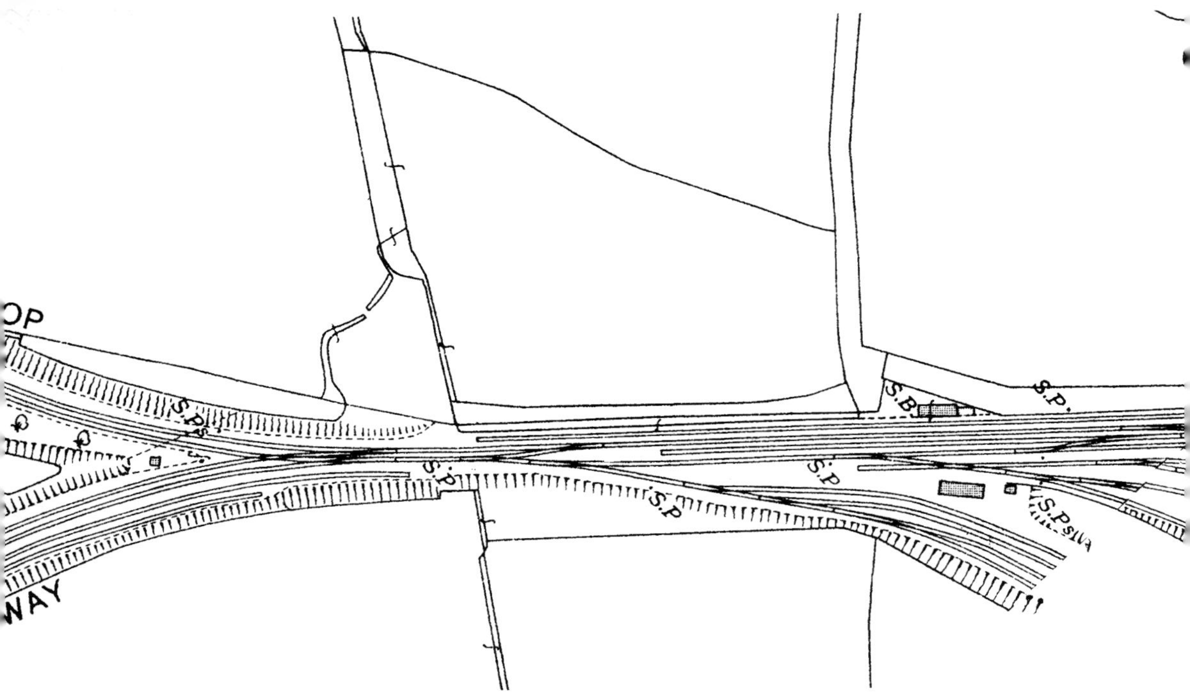

III. The 1905 edition shows the 1902 station complete on the right page and work in progress on the locomotive depot and other sidings. Marked S.B. on the left page is Station signal box.

3. No. 7032 *Denbigh Castle* is waiting to depart for Swansea in about 1960 and is flanked by two of the recently introduced DMUs. The tall chimneys are on the premises of United Dairies, which retained a siding into the 1970s. The centre road was the "Up Goods Loop" and was used until 1972. (W.A.Camwell/SLS coll.)

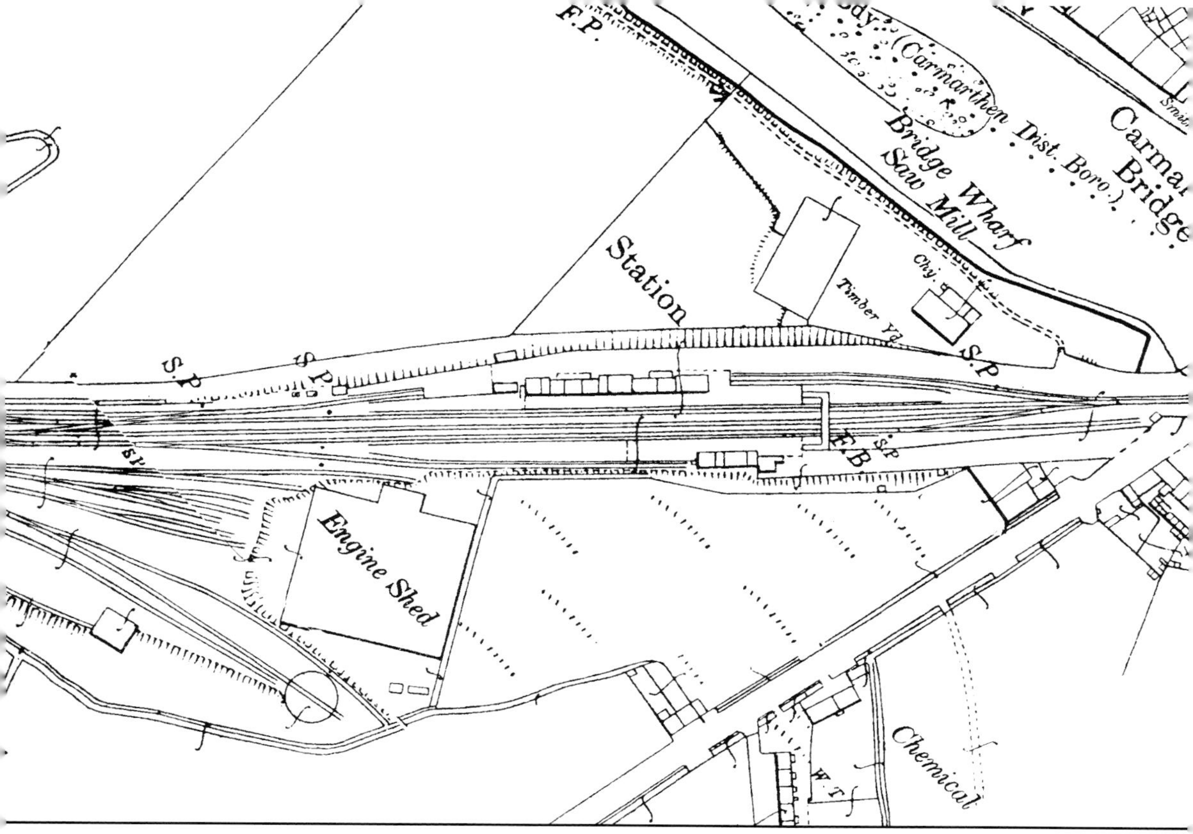

4. Outside the shed on 27th August 1963 were no. 6844 *Penhydd Grange* and no. 5042 *Winchester Castle*. The tall fitting shop was equipped with a travelling crane. The shed was coded 87G and closed on 13th April 1964. (D.A.Johnson)

5. Most of the locomotive depot sidings were abandoned in 1970, but some short lengths were retained for berthing diesels. Resting on 28th April 1984 were nos 37279/296 and 248. The tankers on the right are close to the 1970 siding of the Aberthaw & Bristol Channel Cement Company. There was a private siding on the left for J. Bibby's agricultural supplies. (D.H.Mitchell)

6. No. 6000 *King George V* stands with a special on 5th September 1987 and displays the bell from its North American tour. The colour light signal is one of a batch provided in 1972 and is close to the line used by most trains by that time. (N.W.Sprinks)

↓ 7. A single car was sufficient for many local services by the time no. 153374 was recorded in 1995. The bridge in the background replaced a level crossing in 1938. Crossing Box had been nearby until 15th December 1968. Milk traffic continued north to Lampeter until 1973. (A.C.Mott)

8. No. 59206 had left Paddington at 07.08 on 13th June 2009 with the "Thames-Towy" excursion and is seen shortly after arrival at 12.05. This platform was used by several trains each day by that time and it had gained a shelter and indicator. The loss of the footbridge mattered little, as the lines in the foreground were rarely used. (P.G.Barnes)

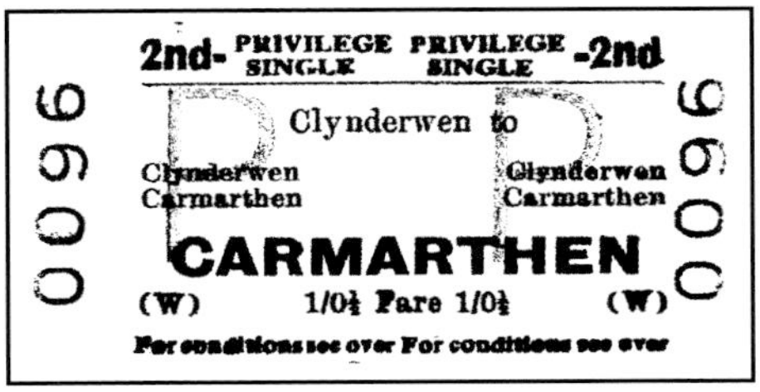

0096
2nd- PRIVILEGE SINGLE PRIVILEGE SINGLE -2nd
Clynderwen to
Clynderwen Carmarthen
Clynderwen Carmarthen
CARMARTHEN
(W) 1/0½ Fare 1/0½ (W)
For conditions see over For conditions see over
0096

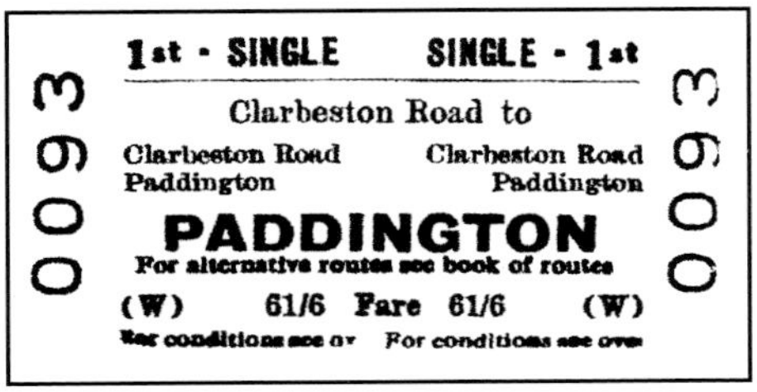

0093
1st - SINGLE SINGLE - 1st
Clarbeston Road to
Clarbeston Road Paddington
Clarbeston Road Paddington
PADDINGTON
For alternative routes see book of routes
(W) 61/6 Fare 61/6 (W)
See conditions see ov For conditions see over
0093

9. The northwest facade of the 1902 buildings was little changed when photographed 107 years after completion. (V.Mitchell)

10. Photographers were allowed to stand on the disused sidings on 25th July 2009 to record the much-admired and newly-built 4-6-2 no. 60163 *Tornado*. The fire brigade had been invited to supply its water needs. (V.Mitchell)

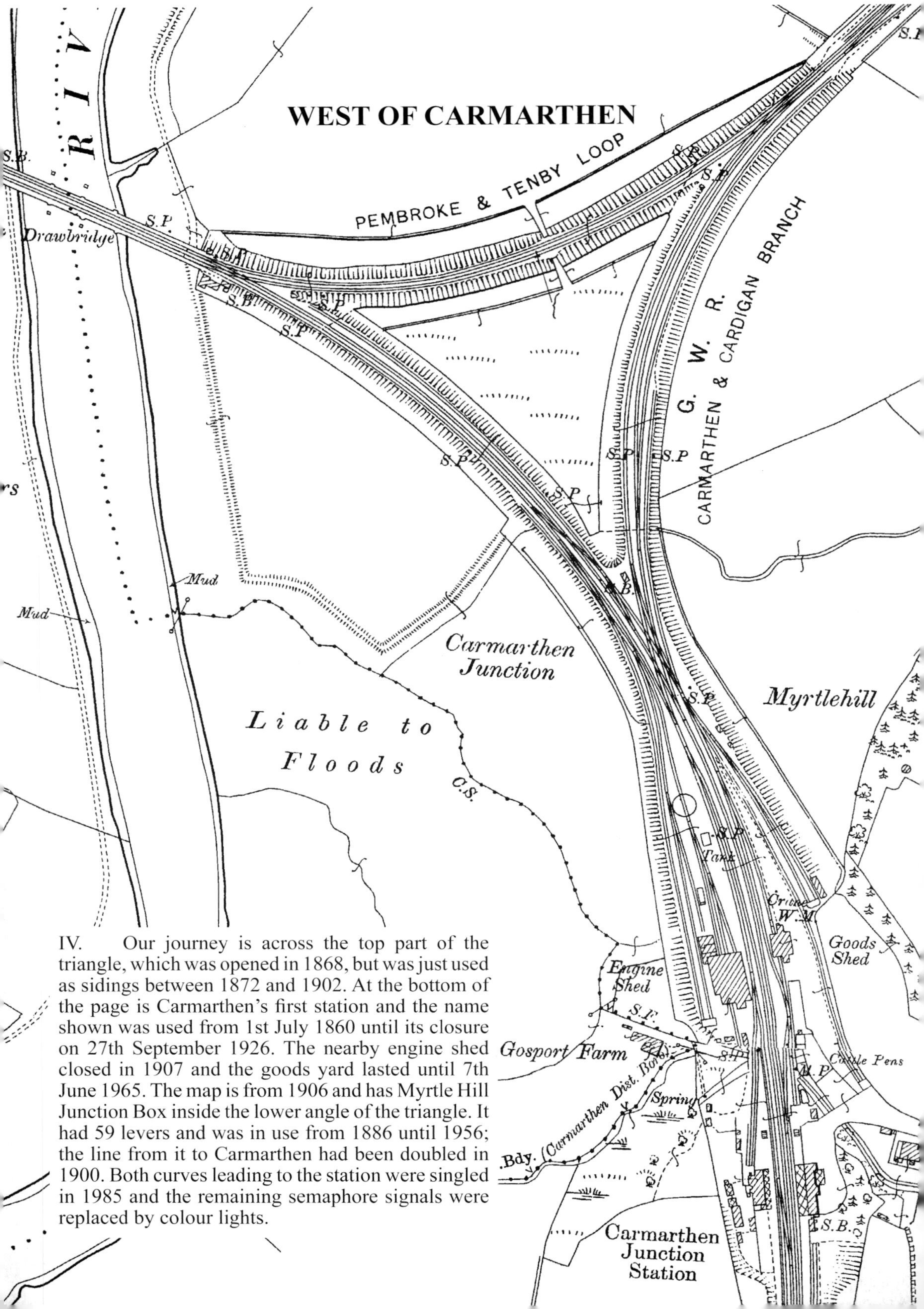

IV. Our journey is across the top part of the triangle, which was opened in 1868, but was just used as sidings between 1872 and 1902. At the bottom of the page is Carmarthen's first station and the name shown was used from 1st July 1860 until its closure on 27th September 1926. The nearby engine shed closed in 1907 and the goods yard lasted until 7th June 1965. The map is from 1906 and has Myrtle Hill Junction Box inside the lower angle of the triangle. It had 59 levers and was in use from 1886 until 1956; the line from it to Carmarthen had been doubled in 1900. Both curves leading to the station were singled in 1985 and the remaining semaphore signals were replaced by colour lights.

11. We are at the top right corner of the map in May 1964, looking towards the present station, with the 1930 carriage sidings on the right and Station Box on the left. The outline of the engine shed is beyond the signals. (P.J.Garland/R.S.Carpenter)

12. This signal box was built east of the southern junction in 1956 and is seen from a down train in July 2009. It controlled the entire triangle from 1972. A panel to operate the colour light signals arrived in 1985. (V.Mitchell)

13. Carmarthen Bridge Box is seen from the bridge approach in May 1964. It had 33 levers and closed on 7th May 1972. The route west to Whitland had one broad gauge track and one standard one from 1868 to 1872. (P.J.Garland/R.S.Carpenter)

14. The first bridge was designed by I.K.Brunel and comprised 13 timber spans and an iron drawbridge. One half of this rolled onto the other half. The total length of all the spans was 385ft. The building of a new bridge took place in 1911. (GWR Magazine)

15. The replacement had six steel spans, one of which lifted. It was of the bascule type, which rolls as it rises. Each side are the counter balance weights, which have dropped into pits. The electric motors had standby hand winches. The bridge came into use on 2nd July 1911. (GWR Magazine)

V. The diagram of the operating gear shows the span down. The dashed lines indicate the up position.

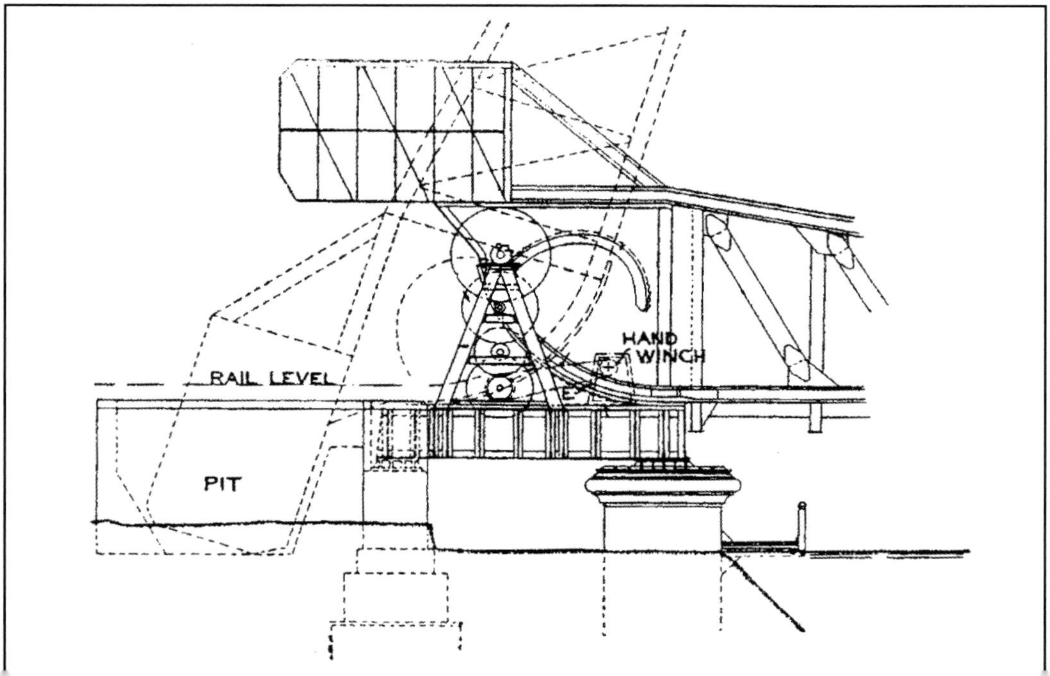

SARNAU

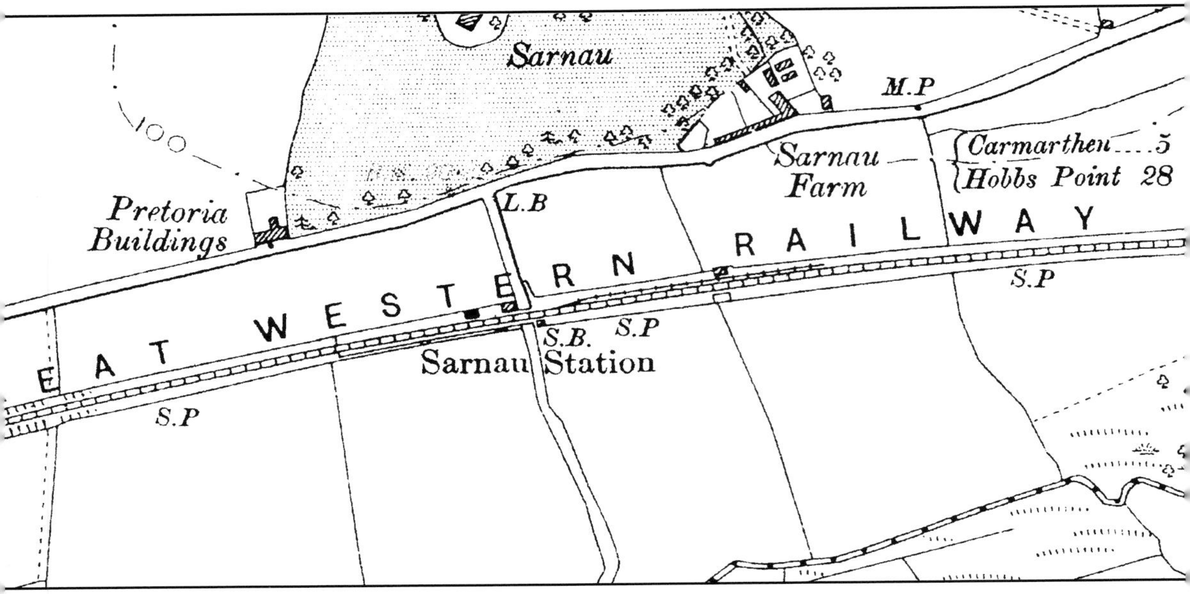

VI. A siding was provided here in 1883, but the station did not open until 6th June 1888. Four miles to the east, there was Llanstephan Crossing, which had a 23-lever signal box until 26th March 1979. Lifting barriers were fitted in 1965 and the crossing was for pedestrians only from 1979. There was a goods loop in use in 1911-65 and a down siding for a creamery from 1934. This is a 12ins to 1 mile map from 1908.

16. An eastward view from 23rd May 1963 includes the signal box, which had a 14-lever frame and was in use until March 1979 when lifting barriers were fitted. In the distance is the small goods shed. The siding formed a loop and was not used after 2nd December 1963. (P.J.Garland/R.S.Carpenter)

17. There had been a staff of four throughout the 1930s, but passenger traffic ceased on 15th June 1964. This photograph shows the other direction on the same day. (P.J.Garland/R.S.Carpenter)

Sarnau	1903	1913	1923	1933
Passenger tickets issued	6128	7026	6844	1043
Season tickets issued	*	*	11	2
Parcels forwarded	6689	20346	16163	7217
General goods forwarded (tons)	95	171	92	29
Coal and coke received (tons)	1731	1321	634	374
Other minerals received (tons)	478	2042	428	696
General goods received (tons)	518	700	541	237
Coal and Coke handled	21	-	223	286
Trucks of livestock handled	-	-	6	20

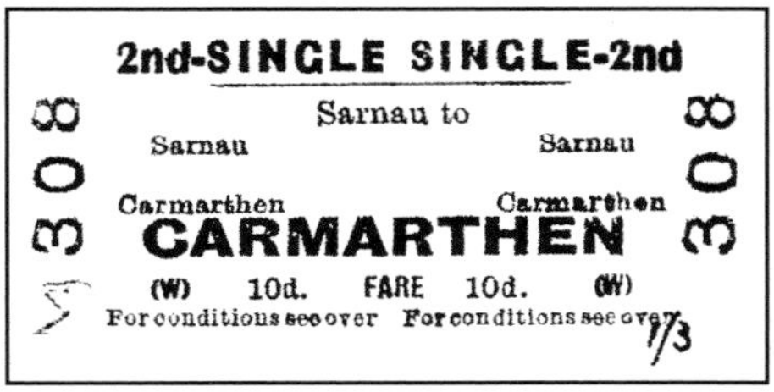
2nd-SINGLE SINGLE-2nd
3308 3308
Sarnau to
Sarnau Sarnau
Carmarthen Carmarthen
CARMARTHEN
(W) 10d. FARE 10d. (W)
For conditions see over For conditions see over
1/3

ST. CLEARS

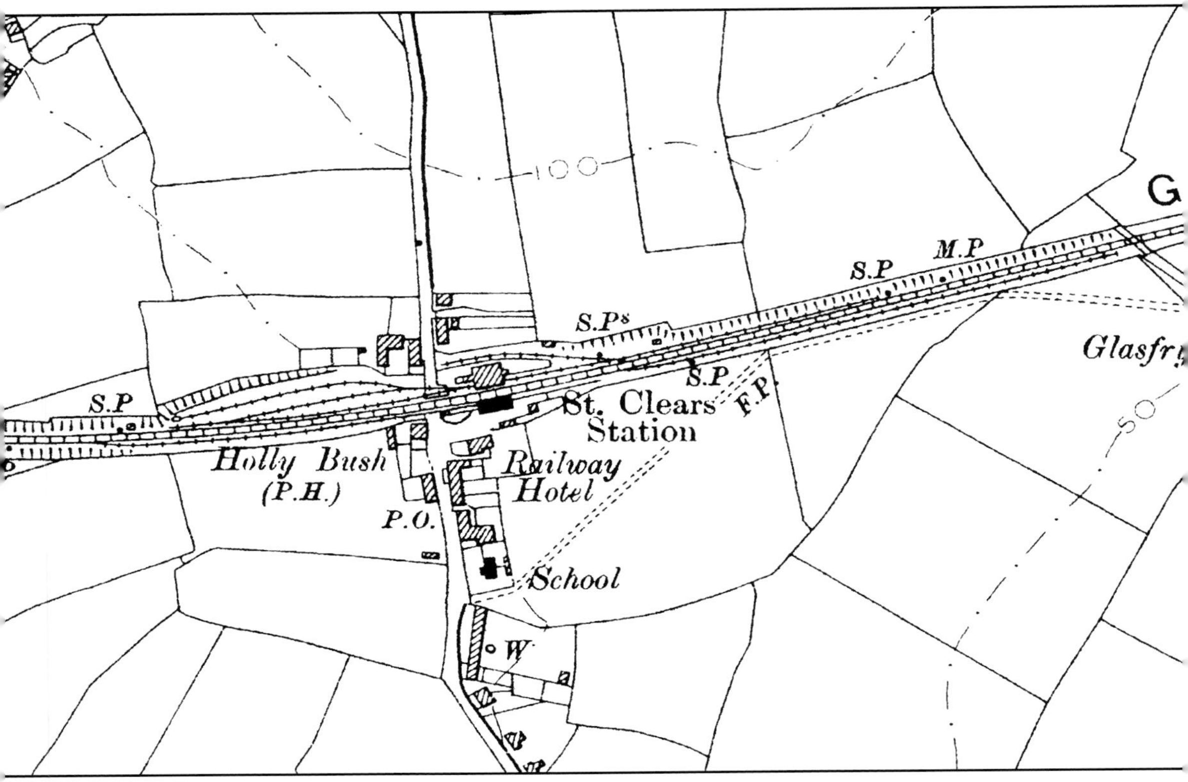

VII. Again, a 1908 map at 12ins to 1 mile shows little evidence of habitation nearby. The population rose from 921 in 1901 to 1937 in 1961.

18. The main building was on the south side of the line and was photographed on 20th October 1904. The staff numbered 12 at that time; it was 15 in 1923 and 13 in 1933. (Lens of Sutton coll.)

19. Looking east in 1958, we see that weather protection on the up side was provided by an economical extension of the goods shed roof. Brunel's influence is evident on the down side. (R.M.Casserley)

St. Clears	1903	1913	1923	1933
Passenger tickets issued	26515	29700	32005	7587
Season tickets issued	*	*	103	83
Parcels forwarded	27122	84613	141725	79385
General goods forwarded (tons)	3282	4649	2834	1130
Coal and coke received (tons)	4399	4243	3577	2318
Other minerals received (tons)	2106	1442	2533	2603
General goods received (tons)	4648	7230	7348	7677
Coal and Coke handled	123	710	1116	1868
Trucks of livestock handled	928	1096	747	390

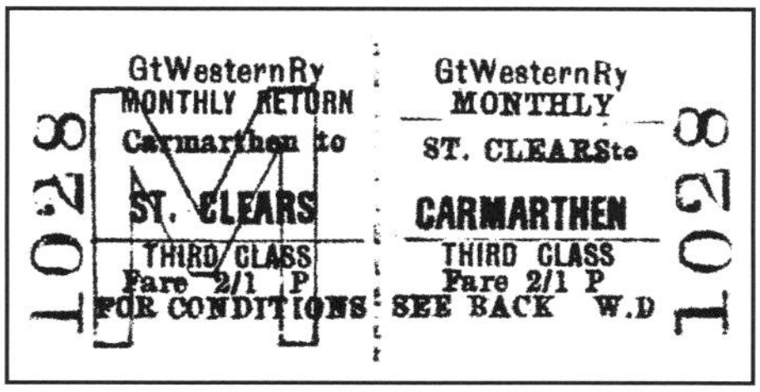

PRIVATE
EKN 557
GUH 464

← 20. A westward panorama from the footbridge on 23rd May 1963 reveals that there were four tracks crossing the road on the level and that there was a down refuge siding. The latter was in use from 1883 until 1966. The goods yard closed on 30th May 1966, its lofty crane being rated at six tons. (P.J.Garland/R.S.Carpenter)

↙ 21. Brunel's chalet styling is more apparent in this 1963 record of the south elevation. Passenger traffic ceased here on 15th June 1964 and Western Welsh buses then had the local monopoly. (P.J.Garland/R.S.Carpenter)

↓ 22. The last scheduled passenger train to Fishguard passed through on 29th September 1965 and it was hauled by no. 6859 *Yiewsley Grange*. It is waiting by the 1882 signal box, which had 28 levers by the time it closed on 12th November 1978. Barriers were installed a few weeks later. (H.C.Casserley)

WHITLAND

VIII. The 1908 survey at 12ins to 1 mile has the Pembroke branch below the main line and its siding, on the left. There were eight such down sidings by 1950, when a turntable was added to the southern one. The engine shed shown was built by the Pembroke & Tenby Railway, which had its own terminal platform nearby until August 1869. The shed burnt down in 1901 and a replacement was brought from Letterston.

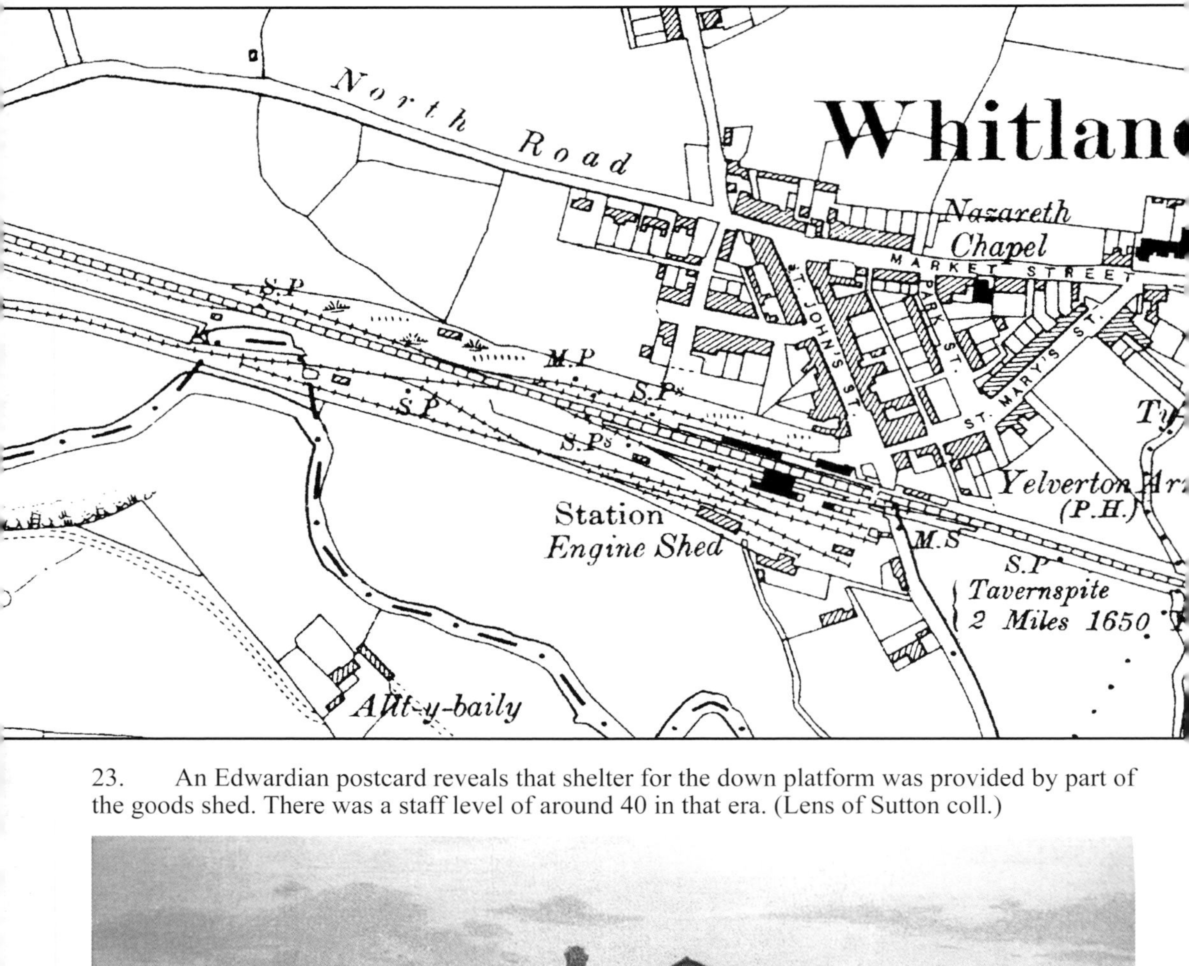

23. An Edwardian postcard reveals that shelter for the down platform was provided by part of the goods shed. There was a staff level of around 40 in that era. (Lens of Sutton coll.)

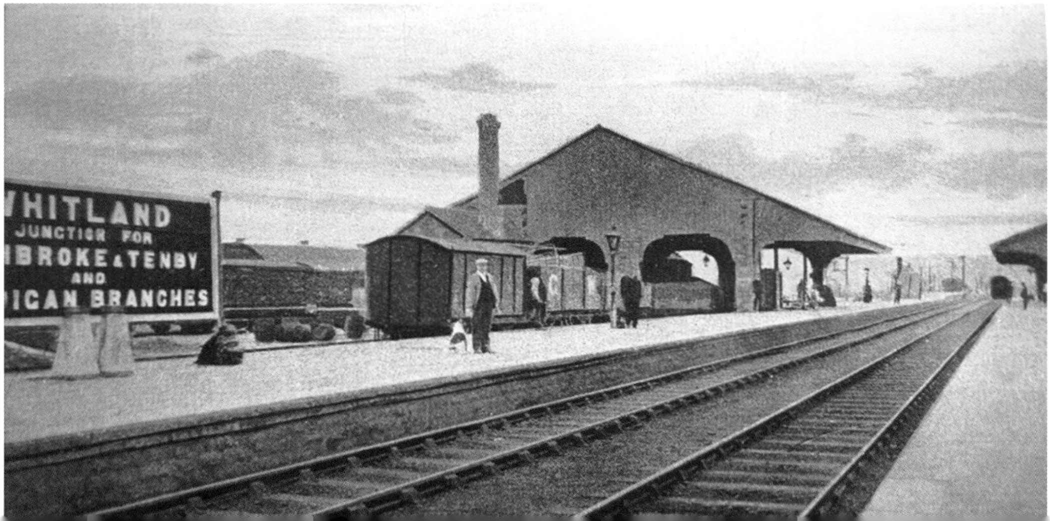

24. The up bay platform is evident in this panorama from the footbridge in the same period. The down bay was just beyond the goods shed and one line served both. Branch trains for both Pembroke and Cardigan generally departed from this bay. (Lens of Sutton coll.)

25. Class 1901 0-6-0PTs were photographed in about 1919, with no. 2012 near the turntable. The GWR code was 517 and it became sub to 87H under BR. There were 19 locomotives allocated here in 1947. (Lens of Sutton coll.)

26. Nos. 4594 and 1613 were on the shed road on 16th June 1960, by which time the structure had been re-roofed. Steam operation ceased here on 9th September 1963 and the shed closed in January 1966. (G.Adams/M.J.Stretton coll.)

27. There had been improvements to the station in 1939 and major rebuilding in 1958. This view west is from 1961, by which time the local population was 1269. The short platform on the left had once carried cattle pens. (R.Dyer/Bentley coll.)

↓ 28. Seen on 24th May 1963 is West Box (43 levers) and the line curving left to Pembroke. The perforated signal arm was for backing purposes. (P.J.Garland/R.S.Carpenter)

29. These sidings west of the station were added by about 1910 and they lasted until 1967. They are seen in 1963, with the Pembroke branch on the extreme right and the turntable road a little nearer. (P.J.Garland/R.S.Carpenter)

Whitland	1903	1913	1923	1933
Passenger tickets issued	33226	40255	38716	23213
Season tickets issued	*	*	56	19
Parcels forwarded	12092	38069	96952	102369
General goods forwarded (tons)	1241	1621	3102	1233
Coal and coke received (tons)	2832	2304	2812	3007
Other minerals received (tons)	1999	1050	3025	1746
General goods received (tons)	3638	4416	4897	4320
Coal and Coke handled	112	574	1243	738
Trucks of livestock handled	593	745	625	497

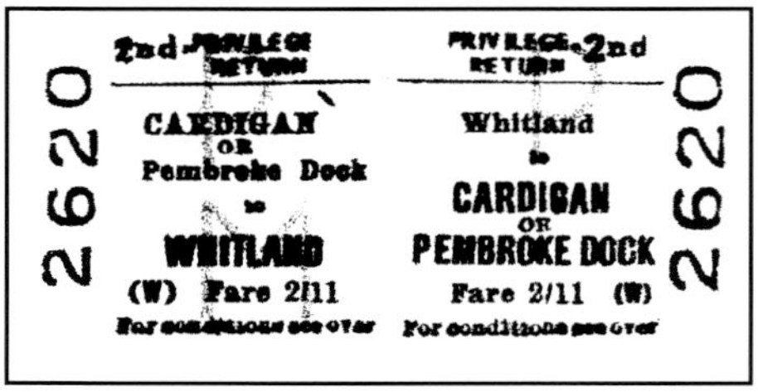
2620
2nd
CARDIGAN
OR
Pembroke Dock
to
WHITLAND
(W) Fare 2/11
2nd
Whitland
to
CARDIGAN
OR
PEMBROKE DOCK
Fare 2/11 (W)
For conditions see over
2620

30. Ready to leave for Pembroke on 26th June 1963 is 2-6-2T no. 5545. The siding on the right formed a loop for many years, passing over the road south of the level crossing gates. (N.K.Harrop/Bentley coll.)

31. Arriving from Carmarthen on the same day is no. 6984 *Owsden Hall*. It is passing East Box (21 levers) having run through the 187yd long Whitland Tunnel, which is almost two miles distant. (N.K.Harrop/Bentley coll.)

32. No. 37190 worked the 07.30 Milford Haven to Swansea on 13th August 1980 and stands beside the 1958 structures, while the down side is awash with water. The up bay ceased to be used by passenger trains in 1972. (D.H.Mitchell)

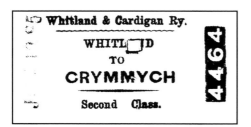

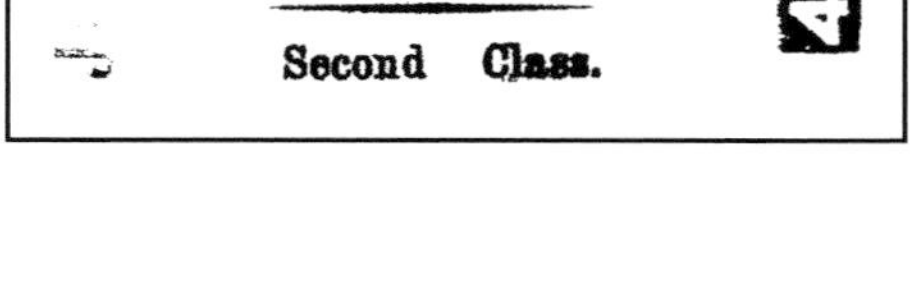
Whitland & Cardigan Ry.
WHITL ID
TO
CRYMMYCH
Second Class.
4464

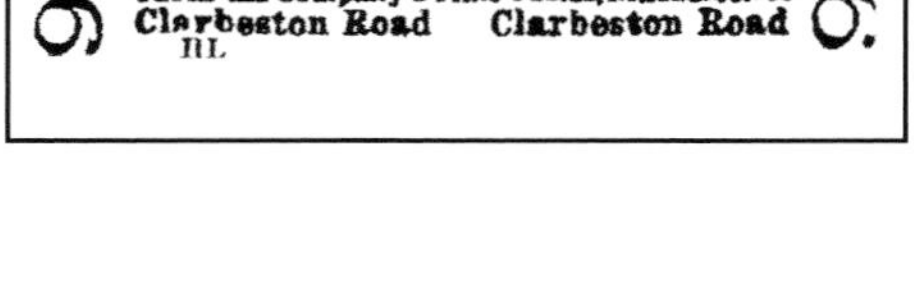
Gt. Western Ry. Gt. Western Ry.
Whitland Whitland
TO
CLARBESTON RD.
1/0 THIRD CLASS 1/0
Issued subject to the conditions & regulations set out in the Company's Time Tables, Bills&Notices
Clarbeston Road Clarbeston Road
9292
9292

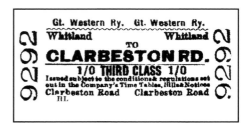

33. The 39-lever signal box served at Danygraig in Swansea Docks from 1959 to 1970 and was one of eight of the 26 built to be relocated. Only Bargoed and Evesham remained in 2010. No. 47254 is hauling the 09.30 Paddington to Pembroke Dock on 27th June 1981. The dairy on the left had its own siding from 1930 until about 1980. (T.Heavyside)

34. Another view from the footbridge on the same day features the 11.35 from Milford Haven to Swansea (right) and a train from Carmarthen (centre) making connection with a Pembroke branch train. (T.Heavyside)

35. An HST operated between London and Pembroke Dock on some Summer Saturdays in 2009 and on 25th July the signalman is seen collecting the single line tablet from the driver. (V.Mitchell)

WEST OF WHITLAND

36. This is Cardigan Junction in May 1963 and the photographer is standing on the branch, which closed on 27th May 1963. The box opened in March 1873 as Taf Vale Junction and was renamed Cardigan Junction in 1896. It had 14 levers and closed on 28th July 1964. (P.J.Garland/R.S.Carpenter)

CLYNDERWEN

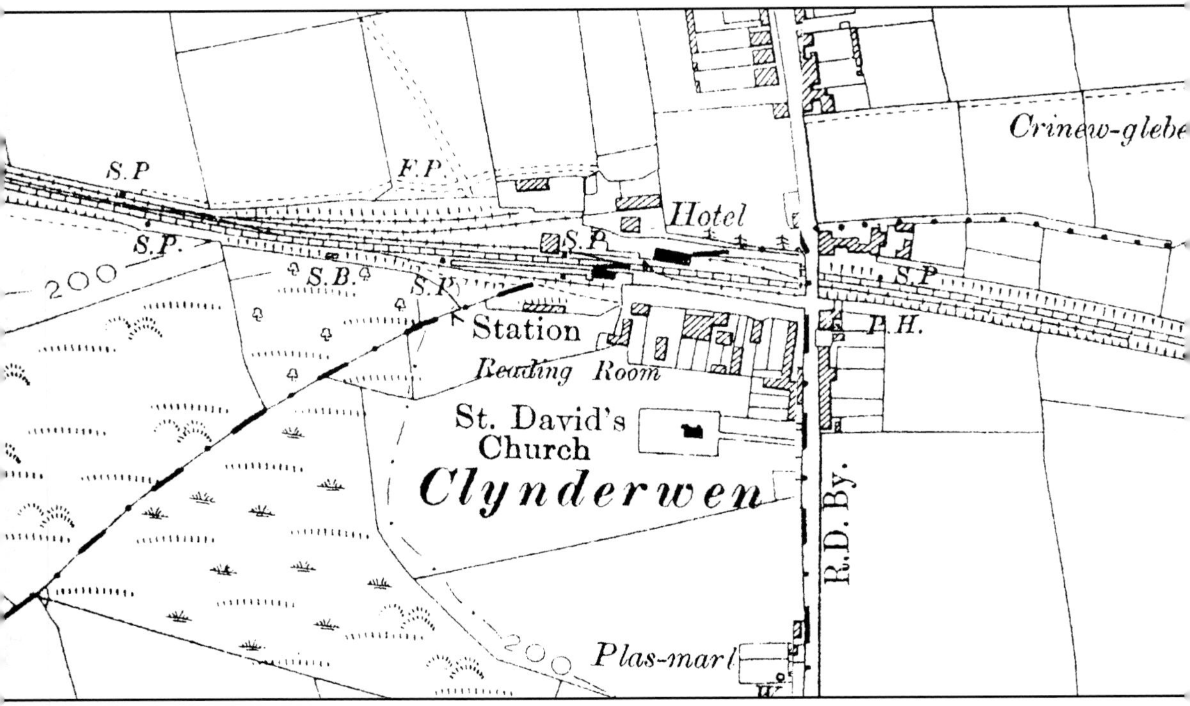

IX. The dots and dashes on this 1908 extract at 12ins to 1 mile reveal that the station was in two counties, the boundary running through the up building. The station was named "Narberth Road" until 1st December 1875. Marked S.B. the 1895 signal box had 41 levers and closed on 3rd October 1966. The upper line on the left ran to Rosebush.

37. A westward panorama in about 1910 includes coacting signals, provided because of visibility limitations created by the bridge on which the photographer is standing. On the left is the down refuge siding, which lasted until 1965. (Lens of Sutton coll.)

38. The manpower increased from seven in 1913 to eleven by 1923. The shed on the right was probably added as an office for the station master. Speeding east in about 1950 is no. 6984 *Owsden Hall*. The ground on the right was the site of a bay platform prior to 1873 and from 1895 until 1917. (W.A.Camwell/SLS coll.)

39. No footbridge was provided, passengers having to traverse complex trackwork, with minimal lighting. The almost flat arch of the road bridge was a Brunelian feature. This and the next view date from 25th May 1963. The crossover was removed in 1966. (P.J.Garland/R.S.Carpenter)

Clynderwen	1903	1913	1923	1933
Passenger tickets issued	12975	13934	14472	10355
Season tickets issued	*	*	50	47
Parcels forwarded	4787	12989	21410	18387
General goods forwarded (tons)	815	1167	518	497
Coal and coke received (tons)	2212	1667	1363	1043
Other minerals received (tons)	1209	632	2360	1791
General goods received (tons)	1508	2303	2900	4525
Coal and Coke handled	16	136	350	347
Trucks of livestock handled	457	452	655	372

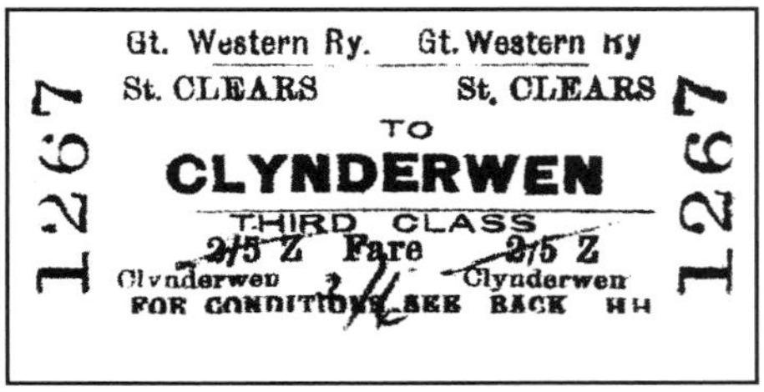

40. In front of the goods shed is a 30cwt crane; the yard closed on 6th September 1965. Brunel's architecture was retained until the official vandals moved in. The fire buckets are hanging on the roofless facilities for gentlemen. (P.J.Garland/R.S.Carpenter)

41. The Fishguard Harbour to Paddington express speeds through on 27th June 1981, hauled by no. 47477. Electric lighting has arrived, but an old post remains along with its oil lamp winch. There was still road access to both platforms. (T.Heavyside)

CLARBESTON ROAD

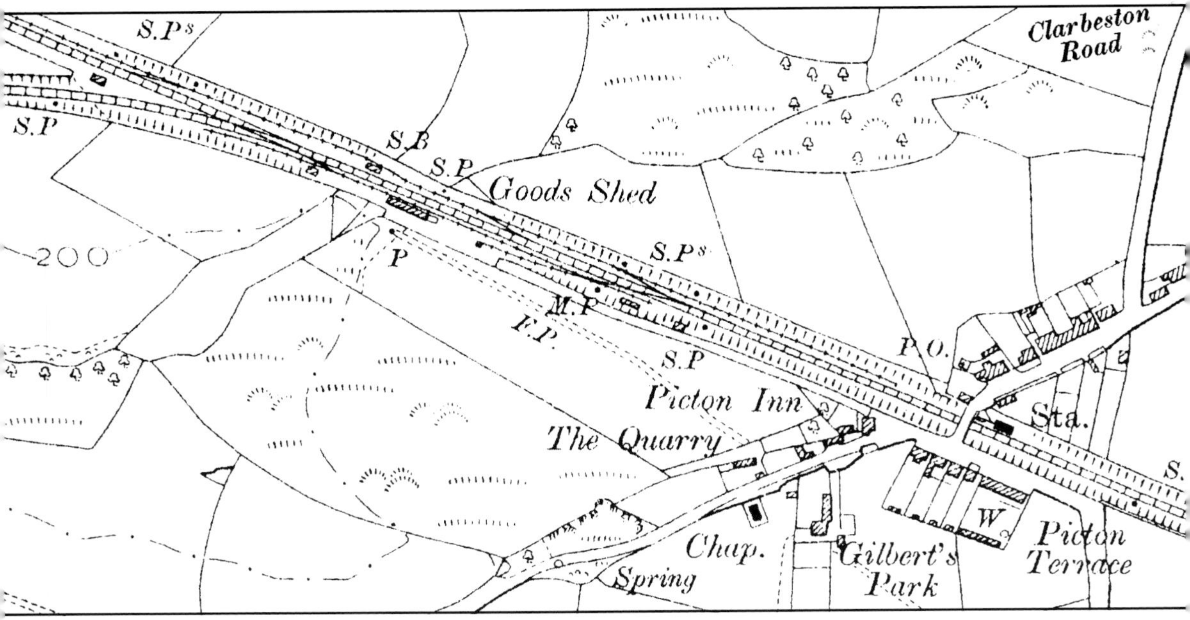

X. The lower line on the left of this 1908 map at 12ins to 1 mile is the route to Haverfordwest. Above it is the 1906 Fishguard line and above that is a long siding. The station was rebuilt west of the road bridge and it opened there on 27th July 1914.

42. A down express has arrived on 6th June 1951, bound for Milford Haven, while the Fishguard autotrain waits ahead of 0-4-2T no. 1431. (A.J.Pike/F.Hornby)

43. The 1914 entrance was recorded on 8th July 1958, along with the photographer's Hillman 10. There were six employees at the old station, but eleven at the new one in most years between the wars. (H.C.Casserley)

44. An eastward view on 22nd June 1963, includes the location of the first station, beyond the bridge. The building seen in the previous picture is beyond this one, up in the trees. The posts carry frames for Tilley pressurised oil lamps. (P.J.Garland/R.S.Carpenter)

45. The western panorama on the same day has the bay signals on the right and the goods yard on the left. This closed on 2nd December 1963; a 30-cwt crane was on hand. (P.J.Garland/R.S.Carpenter)

46. We move west on 26th June 1981 to see the 15.35 Milford Haven to Swansea pass the 1906 signal box, which was termed "East" until 9th July 1923. "West" had been on the line to the left until that time. East had an 80 lever frame fitted in 1914, panels following in 1982 and 1988. The junction was moved a little to the east in 1982 and it is now the end of double track from the east. (T.Heavyside)

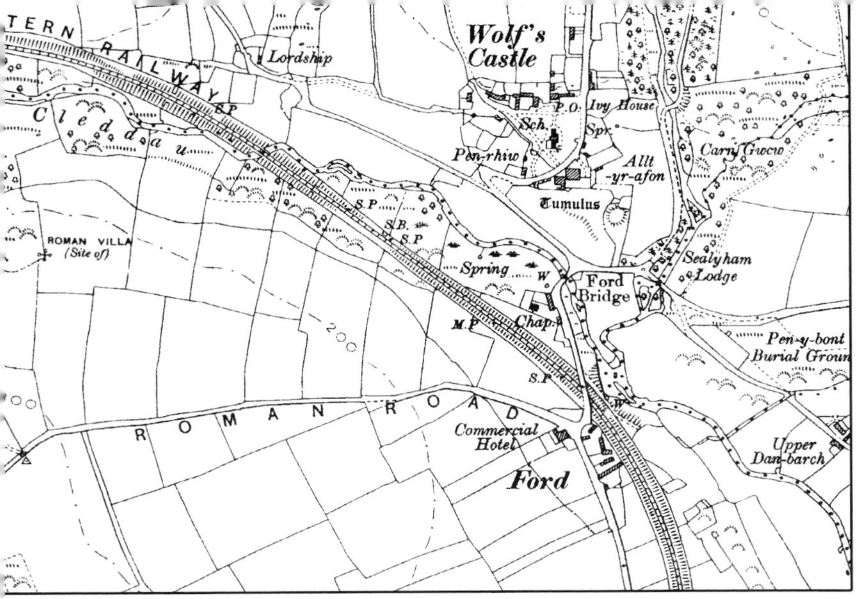

WOLF'S CASTLE HALT

XI. South of this location is Spittal Tunnel (243 yds) and north of it was Treffgarne Quarry, the siding for which was open in 1925-57. The halt opened on 1st October 1913 and is thus not shown on this 1908 survey at 6ins to 1 mile.

47. We look north at the short platforms on 8th July 1958 and see part of the three flights of steps required to enter the cutting. The name is reputed to be associated with the demise of the last wild wolf in Britain. (H.C.Casserley)

48. Recorded on the same day was 0-6-0PT no. 8739 with the 11.15 local train from Clarbeston Road. The suffix to the name is "For Treffgarne Rocks", a local beauty spot. (R.M.Casserley)

WELSH HOOK HALT

XII. We are near the lower left corner of this extract from the 1ins to 1 mile of 1948. The single line running across it is the original steeply graded route to Fishguard; Rosebush is just beyond the right border. Close examination will reveal the goods line passing near Tre-Cŵn, known as Trecwn Siding.

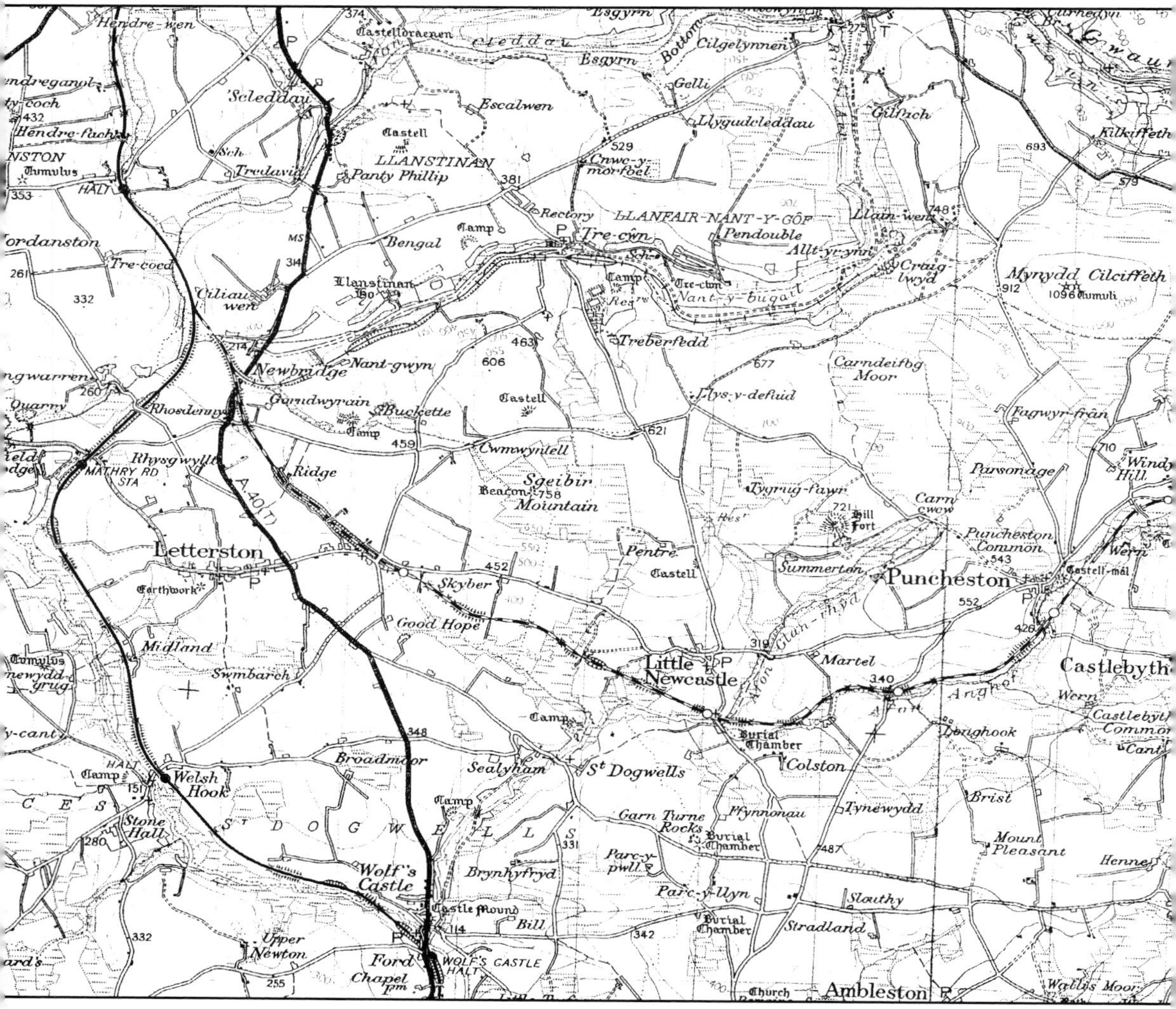

Clarbeston Road	1903	1913	1923	1933
Passenger tickets issued	9050	11100	13264	8465
Season tickets issued	*	*	52	54
Parcels forwarded	4032	7263	6141	7915
General goods forwarded (tons)	131	248	2034	96
Coal and coke received (tons)	1369	1423	866	1098
Other minerals received (tons)	294	1232	194	772
General goods received (tons)	843	1464	1378	1110
Coal and Coke handled	48	136	394	1312
Trucks of livestock handled	151	296	385	350

49. Looking south on 8th July 1958, we can see the reason why autocoaches were fitted with folding steps. The halt came into use on 5th May 1924. "For St. Lawrence" was the suffix. (R.M.Casserley)

50. No. 8739 arrives with the 10.20am Fishguard Harbour to Clarbeston Road on the same day. The halt closed on 6th April 1964, but few would be concerned about concrete sleepers obstructing the down platform. (R.M.Casserley)

MATHRY ROAD

51. The GWR began its service to St. Davids on 1st August 1923 and Burford no. 565 was photographed at about that time. There were three return trips on weekdays. (GWR)

52. This shelter was erected at the crossroads, which was three miles west of the station and close to the village of Mathry. The 10.30am bus continued to Fishguard on Thursdays. (GWR)

53. Opened as Mathry on 1st August 1923, "Road" was added six weeks later. This is the view south on 20th June 1962 and it includes the points of the crossover also evident in the next view. The 14-lever signal box was in use from 23rd November 1925 until 5th September 1965; it had earlier served at Wolf's Castle. (R.G.Nelson/T.Walsh)

54. There was a staff of three throughout the 1930s. Both sidings can be seen in this photograph from 22nd May 1963. The goods yard opened on 20th August 1923 and closed on 2nd December 1963. Passenger service ceased on 6th April 1964. (P.J.Garland/R.S.Carpenter)

LETTERSTON JUNCTION

55. On the left of this southward view from July 1958 is the Trecwn Branch, which formed part of the first route to Fishguard. The double track main line was provided with a loop each side from 1907 until 1938, when two more were laid to the north of them. The signal box was built with a 43-lever frame in 1906 and one with 78 levers was fitted in 1937 in anticipation of the new layout and World War II. (H.C.Casserley)

56. The route was singled on 17th May 1971, but one loop was retained here. This box came from West Drayton West and its 26 levers came into use on 30th July 1972. It closed in 1987, but the loop was retained, with ground frames. No. 33002 waits at the signal with a train to Fishguard on 27th September 1982, while no. 33020 hauls a train from there, without stopping. (P.Jones)

TRECWN BRANCH

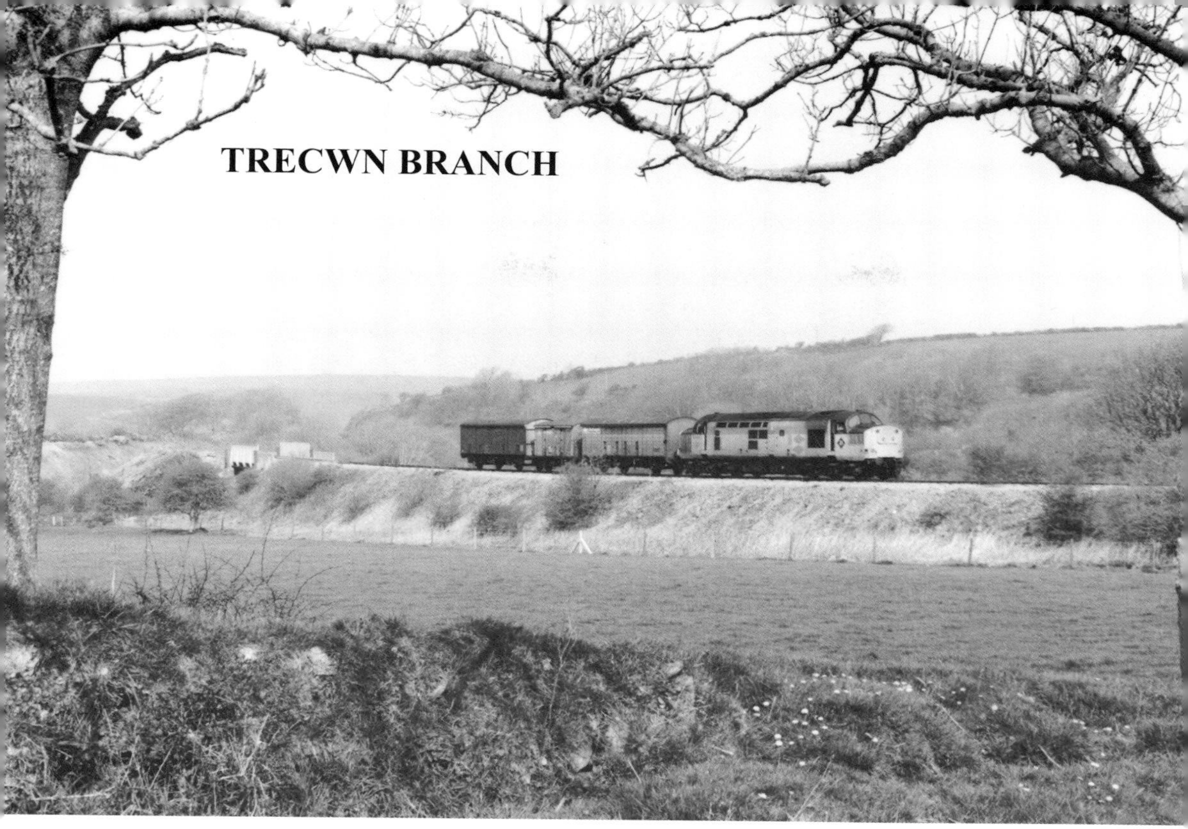

57. This section opened in 1899, but lost its passenger service in 1937. The Army established a camp at Trecwn during the Boer War and World War I to serve as an isolation hospital. A siding was laid to enable servicemen contracting contagious diseases overseas to be conveyed from ships arriving at Fishguard Harbour. The line west of Letterston was retained for general goods until 1st March 1965 and the short length to Trecwn Depot lasted until 1996. Traversing it on 24th April 1990 is no. 37047 with the weekday goods train between Carmarthen and Haverfordwest, which reversed on the loop. (H.Ballantyne)

58. The Royal Naval Armaments Depot was a place of very high security and a railtour on 28th April 1984 reached the gates, but was allowed no further. The locomotive is no. 37189. Workmens trains ran into the depot until 3rd August 1964, these starting at Fishguard Harbour. The word is usually spoken "Treck-oon". (D.H.Mitchell)

TRECWN DEPOT

Trecwn was a long thin depot with narrow gauge (NG) tracks intertwining and going back and forth across the very narrow and deep valley. There were 34 underground explosive storehouses (UES) on the east side of the valley and 24 on the west side. The serial numbers of the UES run from 1 to 59. It appears that there were no nos 47-51. They were at Milford Haven. There were two sizes of UES at Trecwn of 644 cubic metres and 1276 cubic metres. The ravine was much deeper than it is now as all the spoil from the tunnels was used to provide a level floor to the ravine where laboratories and examination houses were built. The main standard gauge (SG) internal line ran quite a way up the east side of the valley and served two SG/NG transfer sheds. There was a SG/NG transfer shed at the bottom of the ravine serving UESs on the west side of the valley. There was a large exchange area just inside the rail gate, which comprised of seven sidings. There were separate SG and NG locomotive sheds adjacent to the exchange sidings.

59. Omega Pacific purchased the former secret ammunition storage depot in December 1997 to service a jet engine refurbishment plant for an associate company. Seldom had photography been allowed, but in August 2003 consent was given for these views of the long disused system. The initial fleet of Hunslet diesel locomotives was replaced by Baguley Drewry products in about 1980. (N.Catford)

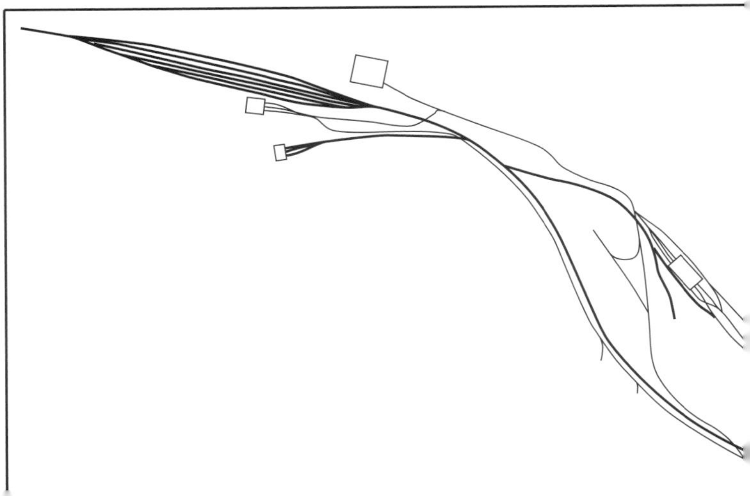

60. The depot was constructed between 1938 and 1942 and the site covers 750 acres. The 58 double skinned underground chambers were mined out of rock and once served by 18 miles of 2ft 6ins gauge railway. All narrow gauge track had been lifted by 2007, but much of the standard gauge material was reported as replaced around 2004. (N.Catford)

The track diagram is shown in its final form. The entrance gates are on the left and the standard gauge lines are shown with a wider line. Most sheds were for transfer purposes, although the two on the left were for engines. There was a UES at the end of each of the short branches.

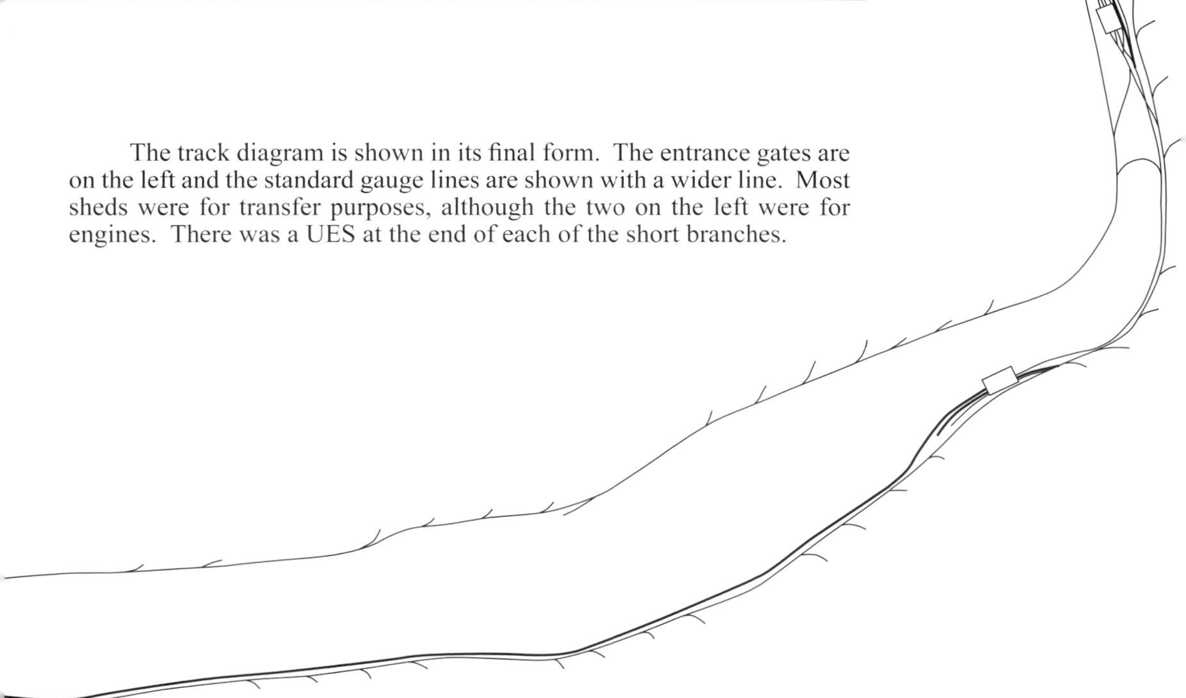

61. Some of the rolling stock was sold and can be seen on lines around Britain, often regauged, but much remained on site. Many vans had opening roofs to allow mines or torpedoes to be loaded from above. On the left of the six sidings are flat wagons with ends; a second batch has been upturned on them. (N.Catford)

62. A similar site existed at Dean Hill and is illustrated in pictures 43 to 57 in our *Hampshire Narrow Gauge* album. The entrance tunnel, the overhead crane in the chamber and platform all appear to be similar. Future uses are few in number, unless you enjoy watching stalactites grow. (N.Catford)

JORDANSTON HALT

63. The line was singled north of Letterston Junction on 9th March 1958 and the former up platform was photographed subsequently. The halt opened on 1st October 1923 and closed on 6th April 1964; it is top left on map XII. (R.M.Casserley)

Iathry Road	1929	1930	1931	1933
'assenger tickets issued	6140	5442	2769	3035
eason tickets issued	3	11	8	3
arcels forwarded	8567	8345	7235	7138
ieneral goods forwarded (tons)	832	1134	480	347
:oal and coke received (tons)	1902	2348	2695	3130
ther minerals received (tons)	1690	1595	1534	1374
ieneral goods received (tons)	2078	2487	3212	3106
:oal and Coke handled	731	782	764	656
'rucks of livestock handled	863	1008	825	778

Fishguard and Goodwick	1903	1913	1923	1933
Passenger tickets issued	8439	17476	20928	23146
Season tickets issued	*	*	35	42
Parcels forwarded	8424	24787	24864	29494
General goods forwarded (tons)	380	1049	1078	428
Coal and coke received (tons)	2156	2330	2698	4631
Other minerals received (tons)	843	1140	1150	1173
General goods received (tons)	2364	5604	7083	5275
Coal and Coke handled	354	4261	6172	3628
Trucks of livestock handled	54	441	562	64

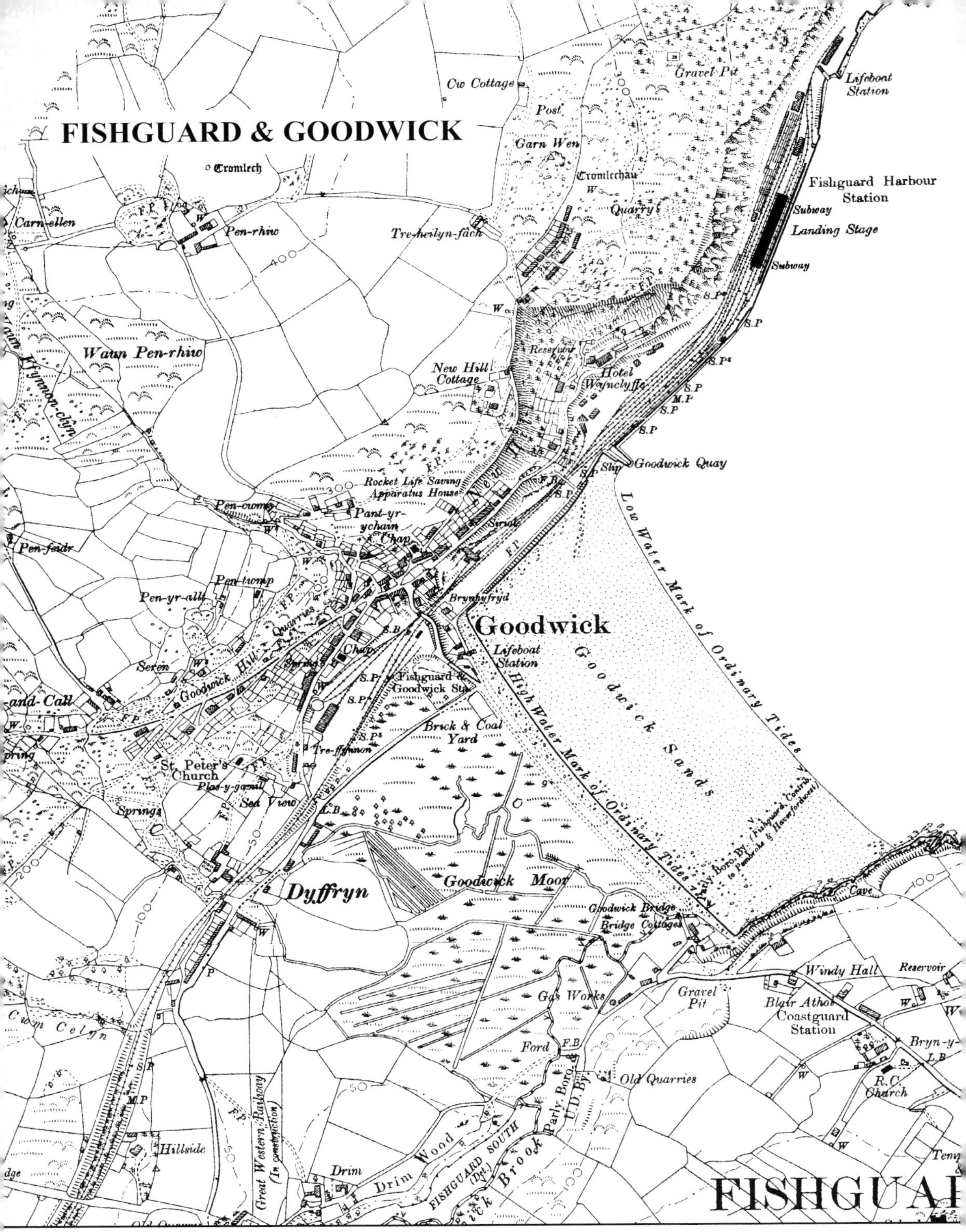

XIII. The 1906 edition at 6ins to 1 mile includes this station, plus the terminus. The northern two miles of the route were never doubled. The orientation of the harbour plus high ground inland give good protection from southwesterly gales. The survey marks the new route as "In construction".

64. This southward panorama has the station on the left and the engine shed centre. Those repairing the chimney (foreground) would have seen across the Irish Sea. The station opened on 1st July 1899, not August as sometimes stated. (Lens of Sutton coll.)

65. An early northward view has the harbour arm in the right background and the goods yard on the left. This soon proved inadequate. There was a staff of four in 1903, this rising to 14 by 1923. (D.Hyde coll.)

66. The engine shed opened in 1906, along with the coal stage (right) which is surmounted by a roofed water tank. The turntable is flanked by the tall curved retaining wall. On the right is 0-4-2T no. 1161 and next to it is no. 2913 *St. Andrew*. The former was withdrawn in 1945 and the latter followed in 1948. The livery suggests the early 1930s. (D.Hyde coll.)

1161

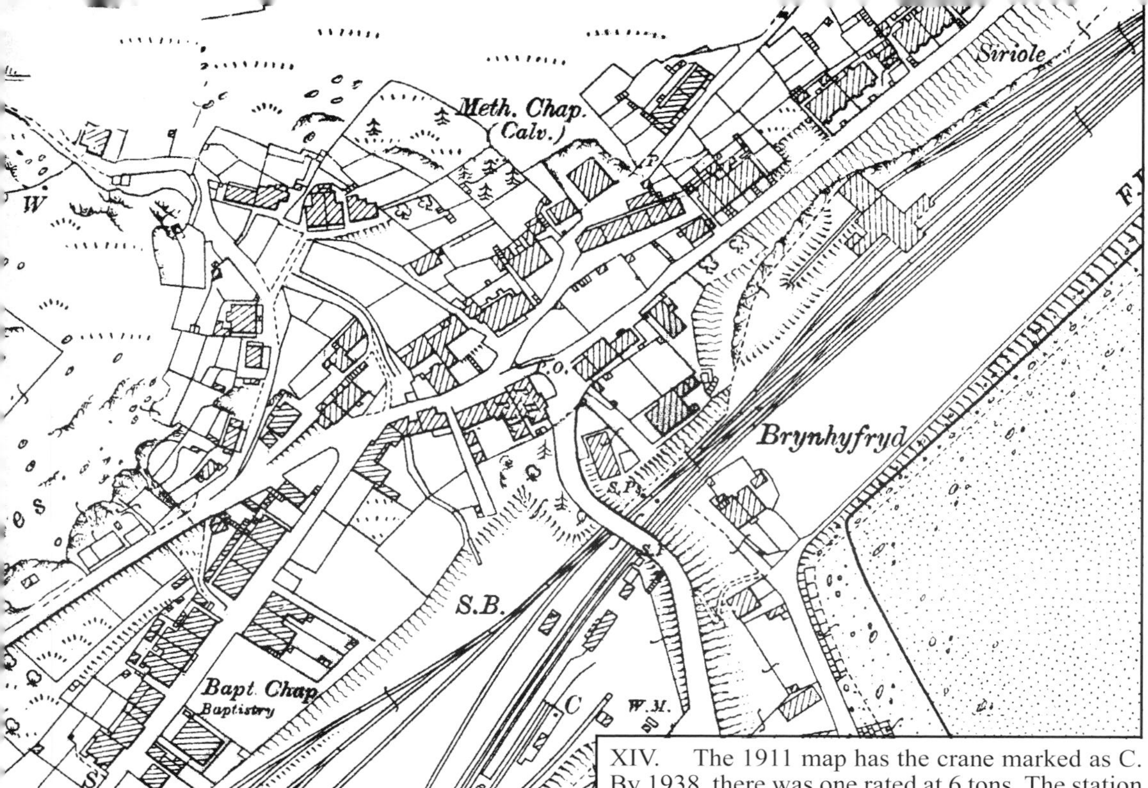

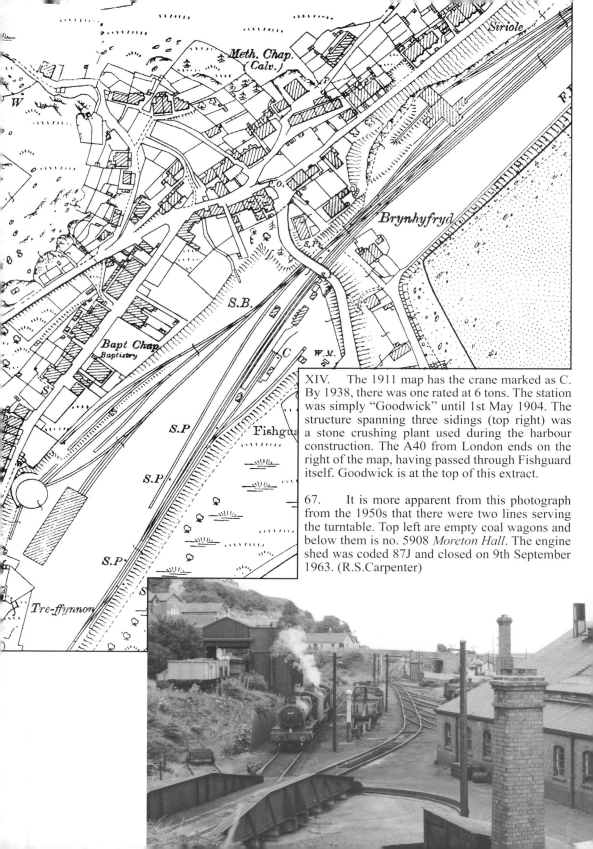

XIV. The 1911 map has the crane marked as C. By 1938, there was one rated at 6 tons. The station was simply "Goodwick" until 1st May 1904. The structure spanning three sidings (top right) was a stone crushing plant used during the harbour construction. The A40 from London ends on the right of the map, having passed through Fishguard itself. Goodwick is at the top of this extract.

67. It is more apparent from this photograph from the 1950s that there were two lines serving the turntable. Top left are empty coal wagons and below them is no. 5908 *Moreton Hall*. The engine shed was coded 87J and closed on 9th September 1963. (R.S.Carpenter)

68. No explanation is available for 0-6-0PT no. 9760 being coupled to railcar no. W11W on 13th June 1954. They are at the down platform, which was added in 1907. (J.H.Bamsey/D.H.Mitchell coll.)

69. This is a view north from the road bridge at the north end of the platforms on 8th July 1958. Lower left is the link to the engine shed. The centre track in the distance was termed the "Down Avoiding Line". (H.C.Casserley)

70. On the right is the original platform of the 1899 terminus; the buildings probably date from that time. The signal box opened on 29th July 1906. The picture is from August 1961. (D.K.Jones coll.)

71. A panorama from the road bridge on 20th June 1962 includes the coal stage (above the brake van) and the engine shed (left of centre). The signal box had 37 levers until a 53-lever frame came from Port Talbot Middle Box in May 1965 to control new Motorail sidings. It was not used after 1983. (R.G.Nelson/T.Walsh)

72. No. 9602 runs in with a stopping train from Clarbeston Road on 25th May 1963. Such local services were withdrawn on 6th April 1964 and only Fishguard Harbour remained open. (E.Wilmshurst)

73. The old buildings were renovated for Motorail traffic and are seen on 25th July 1974. These trains ran seasonally from 19th June 1965 until 16th September 1982. The structure existed in 2009 in a shabby state. (J.Mann/Ted Hancock coll.)

74. No. 47541 is bound for Swansea on 26th June 1981 and is running on a reversible line created in May 1965. The track on the right was termed "Car Ferry Loop" and was also reversible. On the left is a long siding with a short loop. (T.Heavyside)

75. Comparison with pictures 69 and 74 shows that the sole remaining track was moved close to the foot of the cliff to give more space for the motorist. The work was done between 7th June and 4th July 1982; during this period, the station shown above was reopened. The photograph is from 10th September 2000. (Ted Hancock Books)

FISHGUARD HARBOUR

76. The GWR moved its ferry services from Neyland when this station came into use on 30th August 1906. Rosslare and Waterford became the main destinations; Cork was served until 1968. (Lens of Sutton coll.)

77. Another postcard from the initial years and this reveals the magnitude of the anticipated traffic. It did materialise and this was when all of Ireland was still part of the United Kingdom. The staff numbered 74 in 1929 and 101 in 1936. (Lens of Sutton coll.)

78. In addition to passengers, extensive provision was made for cattle. Meat had to be conveyed live in the pre-refrigeration days. The accommodation later received roofing. The biggest crane could lift 21 tons. (D.Hyde coll.)

Fishguard Harbour	1913	1923	1929	1933
Passenger tickets issued	27465	7844	21882	13983
Season tickets issued	*	5	9	4
Parcels forwarded	15897	2272	3228	2890
General goods forwarded (tons)	2243	1849	1167	1162
Coal and coke received (tons)	142	352	-	-
Other minerals received (tons)	130	45	354	18
General goods received (tons)	2540	1867	2112	10393
Coal and Coke handled	67989	18462	1690	156
Trucks of livestock handled	42	582	119	61

79. Excavation at the foot of the cliff was still continuing when this early panorama was recorded. The cattle sheds in the foreground had increased in number from the previous view. The path for imported animals is at the bottom, while construction work continued on the left. (D.Hyde coll.)

80. This superior postcard was sent on 22nd September 1911 and features the marine workshops, plus the massive harbour arm, with a ship at the Ocean Quay. This is another view from the cliff top. (M.Dart coll.)

81. Cunard transatlantic liners sometimes called off shore and tenders were used to transfer some of the passengers. "Bulldog" class 4-4-0 no. 3402 *Jamaica* is piloting one such connecting train, which would give an early arrival in London. The service was between 1906 and 1914, but very irregular. (SLS coll.)

↙ 82. This photograph was taken from the footbridge near Goodwick Quay (shown on map XIII) in the early 1950s. Shunting is 0-6-0PT no. 5716. The coaches on the right are probably sleeping cars, and beyond them is the 65-lever signal box, which had originally served at Reading. It closed on 3rd January 1965, after which time the remaining six sidings were worked from a ground frame. There had been a passenger service to Waterford two or three times per week, but it was withdrawn in 1959. (R.S.Carpenter)

↑ 83. No. 6859 *Yiewsley Grange* heads an RCTS/SLS special train on 26th September 1965. The other three through platforms had been converted to six bays long before this and they were soon to vanish. On the left is the cattle platform and shed. (R.F.Roberts/SLS coll.)

84. Looking south from the sole surviving platform on 15th September 1973, we see the remaining sidings. Adjacent to the one on the right is the former horse platform, by that time used as the Motorail terminal, a function it performed until 1976. All the sidings were removed in 1981 and the running line slewed to the right in July 1982. Lifting barriers were fitted in 1973. (D.H.Mitchell)

85. The "Boat Train" is seen on 13th February 2009 and was the only train of the day west of Clarbeston Road. It arrived at 13.15 and departed at 13.27. There was another train in the middle of the night, also to and from Cardiff. Only a loop remained, but it was seldom used. One could reach Rosslare by ferry in 3½ hours or 1½ hours by catamaran. (V.Mitchell)

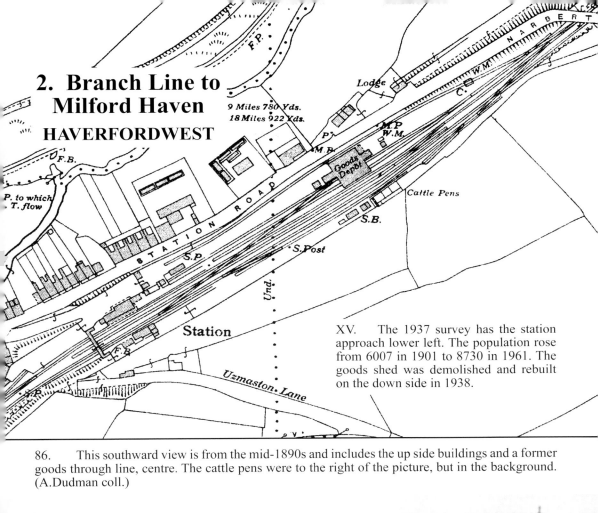

2. Branch Line to Milford Haven

HAVERFORDWEST

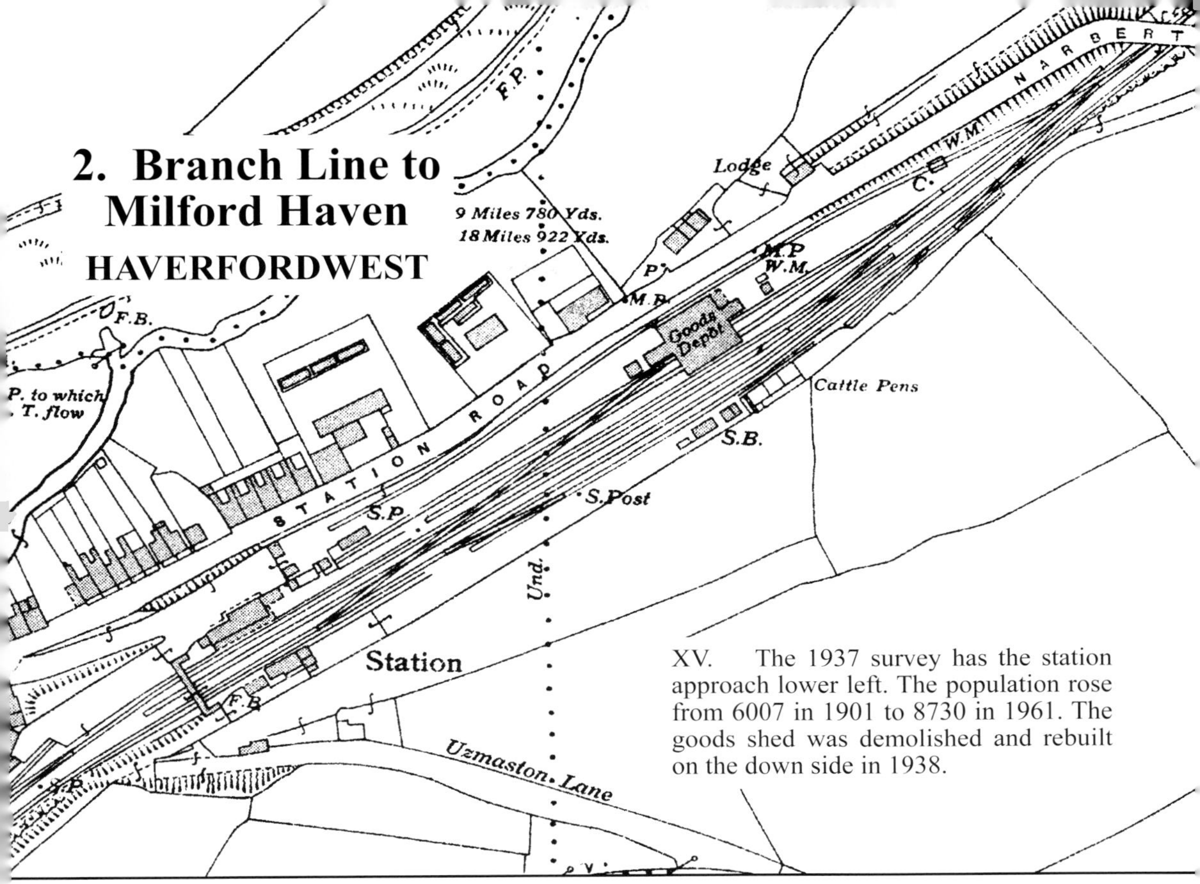

XV. The 1937 survey has the station approach lower left. The population rose from 6007 in 1901 to 8730 in 1961. The goods shed was demolished and rebuilt on the down side in 1938.

86. This southward view is from the mid-1890s and includes the up side buildings and a former goods through line, centre. The cattle pens were to the right of the picture, but in the background. (A.Dudman coll.)

87. An up train waits to depart north on a local service behind no. 5937 *Stanford Hall*, in the late 1950s. Both platforms can still accommodate 13 coaches. (W.A.Camwell/SLS coll.)

88. New buildings were provided on the up side in 1938 and the footbridge was repositioned and reorientated. Its roof is visible on the left of this 1958 photograph. (H.C.Casserley)

↓ 89. We look south on 22nd May 1963 at the extent of the main goods yard (left). Traffic continued into the 1980s when the nearer tracks were lost. The further sidings eventually became the responsibility of EWS. The yard had a 6-ton crane listed in 1938. (P.J.Garland/R.S.Carpenter)

90. A DMU is departing north on a Milford Haven to Carmarthen service on 30th March 1978, while empty tankers destined for the former wait; however, they stand on the reinstated up goods line. The down one is to the right of the down platform, which had been repositioned in 1938. (H.Ballantyne)

➔ 91. The signal box came into use on 12th September 1938 and had 55 levers. No. 33022 is accelerating the 08.27 Milford Haven to Swansea train on 7th September 1983. The box closed on 4th September 1988, following singling of the branch. (H.Ballantyne)

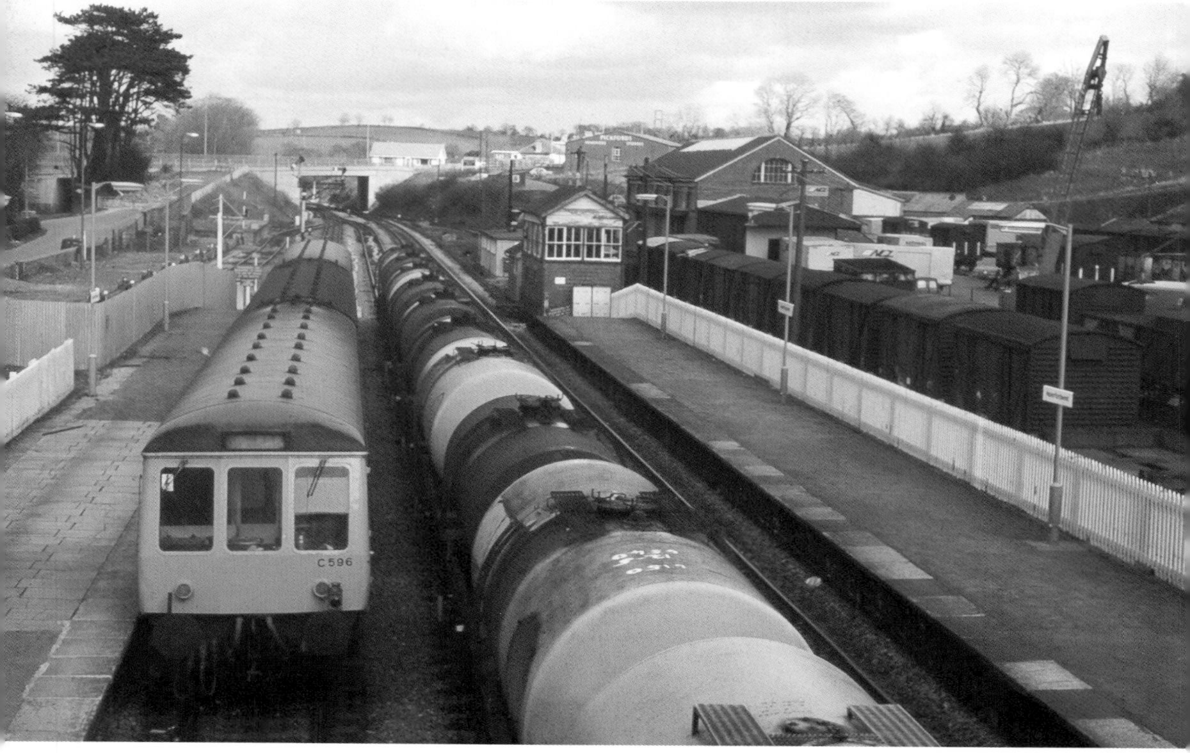

045
Gt. Western Ry. Gt. Western Ry.
FISHWORKER
Milford Haven Milford Haven
TO
BRIXHAM
Via Severn Tunnel
THIRD CLASS
Issued subject to the conditions&regulations set out in the Company's Time Tables, Bills, & Notices
Brixham Brixham
045

Haverfordwest	1903	1913	1923	1933
Passenger tickets issued	50934	54416	57585	17968
Season tickets issued	*	*	265	54
Parcels forwarded	36304	60370	70460	97818
General goods forwarded (tons)	5006	4664	4021	2475
Coal and coke received (tons)	7907	7456	4301	6192
Other minerals received (tons)	1392	1872	4456	5005
General goods received (tons)	11165	10623	17613	20680
Coal and Coke handled	2179	2415	5983	4419
Trucks of livestock handled	1191	991	835	687

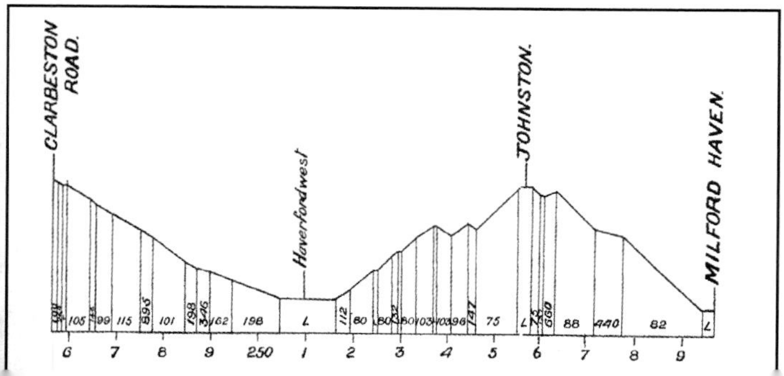

0137
2nd - FORCES LEAVE WEEK-END
FORCES LEAVE - 2nd WEEK-END
Haverfordwest to NEWCASTLE-on-TYNE CENTRAL
via Gloucester and Sheffield
For alternative routes see book of routes
For alternative routes see book of routes
(W) Fare 87/0
Fare 87/0 (W)
For conditions see over
0137

↓ 92. No. D1015 *Western Champion* is seen with the "Pembroke Coast Express" railtour, which started from Paddington at 07.33 on 27th October 2007. The first HST service from here began on 5th September 1983 with an 06.00 departure for Paddington. These loops, plus the one beyond the down platform, were still usable in 2010 and were controlled from Clarbeston Road. (P.G.Barnes)

SOUTH OF HAVERFORDWEST

93. Haverfordwest Bridge is over the Western Cleddau and is 58yds in length. The middle span was last opened in 1968 and the adjacent signal box was closed on 20th April 1970. No. 47432 is bound for Milford Haven on 26th June 1981. (T.Heavyside)

➔ XVI. The 1908 map at 6ins to 1 mile has the double track main line from Haverfordwest to Neyland top left to lower right. The colliery line (top right) was in use in 1901-11. The Hook Anthracite Colliery opened a track on a similar alignment, but with access from the north, in September 1931. It was in use until 1941, when it was taken over to serve a Royal Naval Armaments Depot. The connection lasted until May 1968. Inset is the station area at double size. The name was "Milford Road" in 1859-63. The suffix (Pem.) was added in 1928 and changed to "Dyfed" in 1976. The Neyland line became the branch and it closed to regular traffic on 15th June 1964.

JOHNSTON

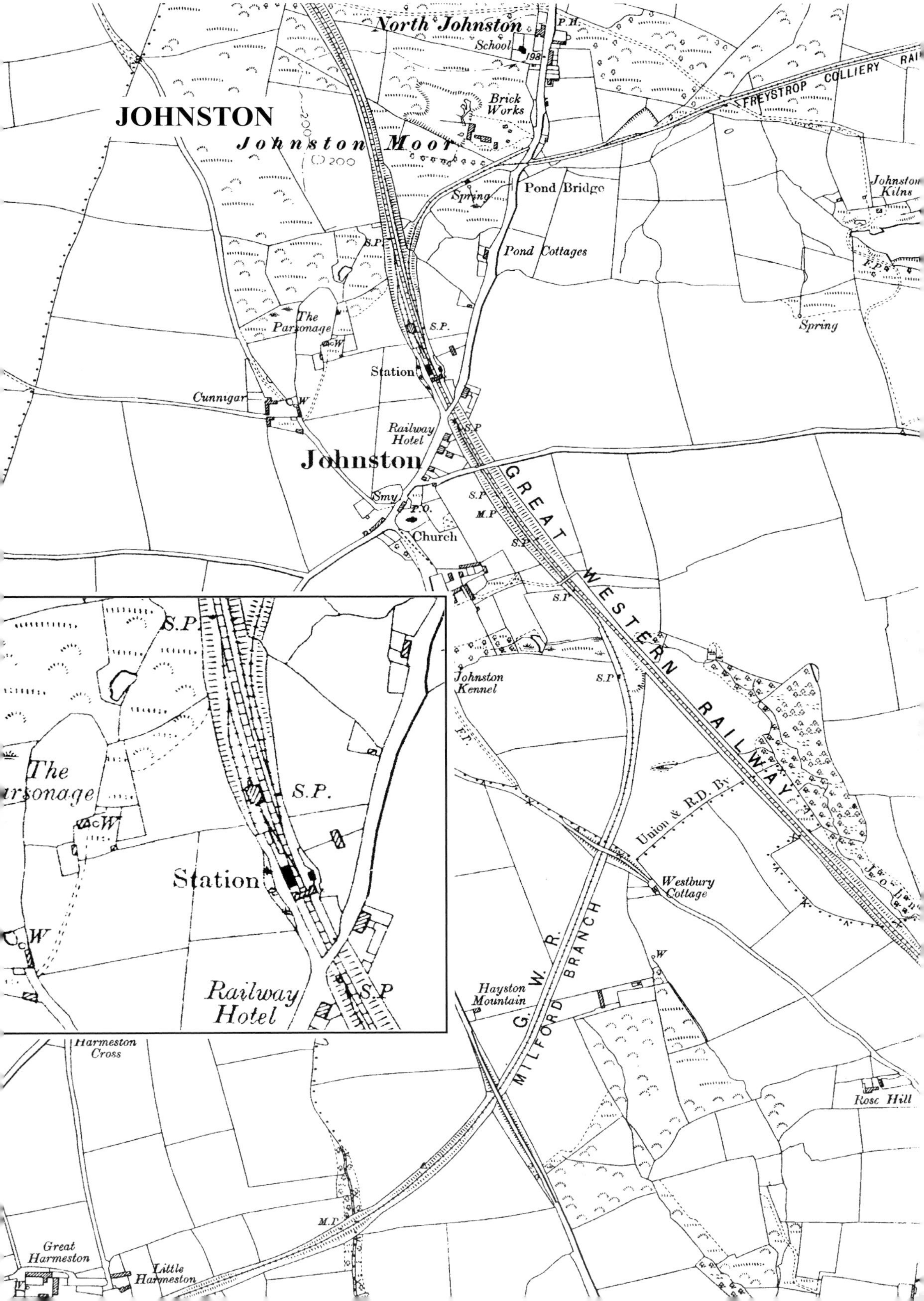

North Johnston
P.H.
School
198
Brick Works
FREYSTROP COLLIERY RAIL
Johnston Moor
200
Pond Bridge
Spring
Johnston Kilns
Pond Cottages
S.P.
F.P.
Spring
The Parsonage
W
Station
Cunnigar
Railway Hotel
Johnston
Smy
P.O.
Church
M.P.
GREAT WESTERN RAILWAY
Johnston Kennel
Union & R.D. By
Westbury Cottage
G. W. R.
MILFORD BRANCH
Hayston Mountain
Rose Hill
Harmeston Cross
Great Harmeston
Little Harmeston

94. The Milford Haven branch train is seen in about 1951 with 0-6-0PT no. 9652 in charge. The station recorded a staff of 9 in 1903 and 1937, but 13 in 1931-34. (R.S.Carpenter)

➔ 95. No. 3654 is working the 7.05pm to Neyland on 7th July 1958. The trolley on the right is for the track gang and the vans are for fish. (H.C.Casserley)

Johnston	1903	1913	1923	1933
Passenger tickets issued	14423	14437	18118	4419
Season tickets issued	*	*	78	-
Parcels forwarded	2134	3087	14677	4617
General goods forwarded (tons)	1431	2222	1691	666
Coal and coke received (tons)	1783	2048	995	1803
Other minerals received (tons)	370	344	1064	803
General goods received (tons)	1109	2774	1951	2252
Coal and Coke handled	195	225	919	4617
Trucks of livestock handled	163	223	239	306

➔ 96. The scene on 22nd June 1960 includes no. 6909 *Frewin Hall* and a DMU, destination Bristol TM. The tracks were signalled for reversible running from 1935. (G.Adams/M.J.Stretton coll.)

JOHNSTON

6909

97. Shunting on the same day is 2-8-0 no. 90225. This was one of a large batch of Ministry of Supply "Austerity" locomotives introduced in 1943 and purchased by BR in 1948. The goods yard closed on 11th January 1965. (G.Adams/M.J.Stretton coll.)

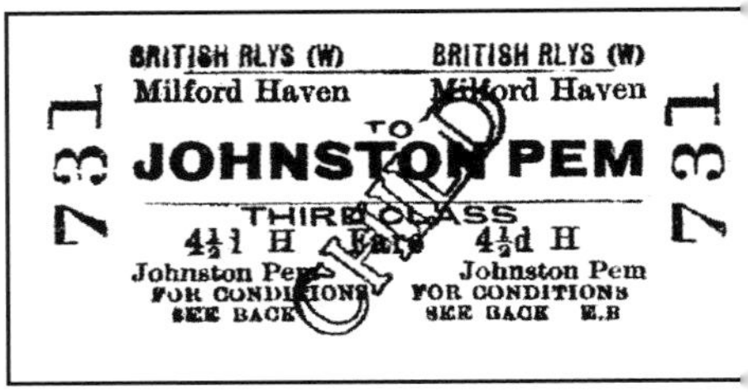
BRITISH RLYS (W)
Milford Haven
TO
JOHNSTON PEM
THIRD CLASS
4½d H Fare 4½d H
Johnston Pem
FOR CONDITIONS SEE BACK
BRITISH RLYS (W)
Milford Haven
Johnston Pem
FOR CONDITIONS SEE BACK E.B
731
731

98. The station became unstaffed on 28th September 1964 and the up platform was still in use in 2010. This and the next view date from 22nd May 1963. (P.J.Garland/R.S.Carpenter)

99. The centre pivot signal was unusual, as was the means of moving the more remote points with double wires, instead of rods. West Box had been near the junction from 1917 until 1935, when this continental system was introduced here. This box lost its suffix and was enlarged to take 44 levers. The wires were used until 1958 and the box closed on 21st August 1988. The line on the right was termed the exchange siding, but was used for splitting down goods trains. (P.J.Garland/R.S.Carpenter)

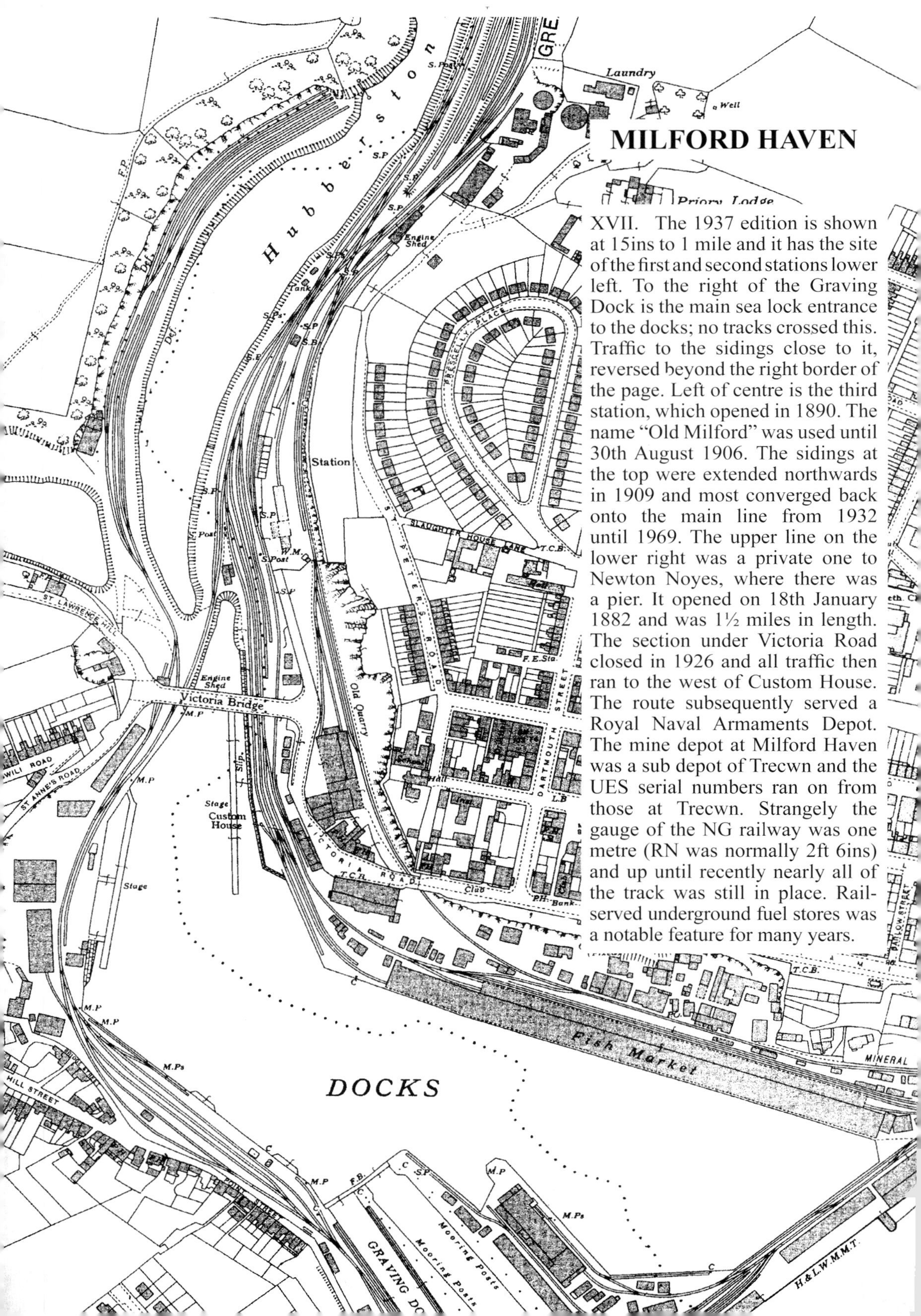

MILFORD HAVEN

XVII. The 1937 edition is shown at 15ins to 1 mile and it has the site of the first and second stations lower left. To the right of the Graving Dock is the main sea lock entrance to the docks; no tracks crossed this. Traffic to the sidings close to it, reversed beyond the right border of the page. Left of centre is the third station, which opened in 1890. The name "Old Milford" was used until 30th August 1906. The sidings at the top were extended northwards in 1909 and most converged back onto the main line from 1932 until 1969. The upper line on the lower right was a private one to Newton Noyes, where there was a pier. It opened on 18th January 1882 and was 1½ miles in length. The section under Victoria Road closed in 1926 and all traffic then ran to the west of Custom House. The route subsequently served a Royal Naval Armaments Depot. The mine depot at Milford Haven was a sub depot of Trecwn and the UES serial numbers ran on from those at Trecwn. Strangely the gauge of the NG railway was one metre (RN was normally 2ft 6ins) and up until recently nearly all of the track was still in place. Rail-served underground fuel stores was a notable feature for many years.

100. The signal box had a 52-lever frame fitted in September 1932 and closure came on 16th December 1973. Passing it sometime in the 1950s is no. 5027 *Farleigh Castle*. (W.A.Camwell/SLS coll.)

101. The railway was closely associated with the fishing industry (note the size of the fish market on the map). This view from 8th July 1958 shows only part of the extensive waterfront. A staff of 44 was required for most of the 1930s. (R.M.Casserley)

102. The small shed housed two engines in 1947 and was then coded Sub to NEY and later Sub to 87H. It is seen in October 1959 and it closed in December 1962. (P.J.Kelley)

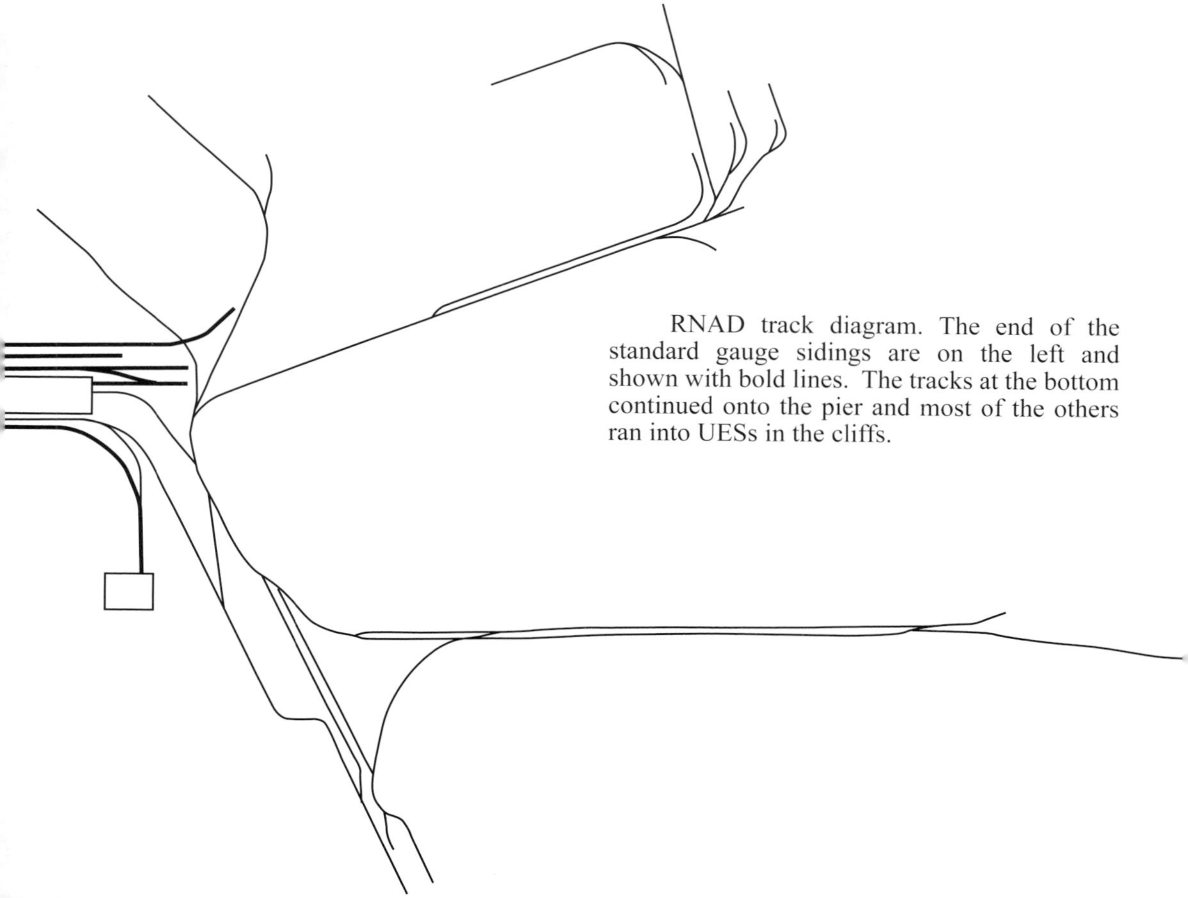

RNAD track diagram. The end of the standard gauge sidings are on the left and shown with bold lines. The tracks at the bottom continued onto the pier and most of the others ran into UESs in the cliffs.

103. Spare couplings hang under the Rochester gas lamp on 22nd June 1960 as 0-6-0PT waits to leave. Out of view on the left stood the massive 6-ton crane. (G.Adams/M.J.Stretton coll.)

104. Fish and ships were the main items encountered in this area, but there was a diesel distraction to attract the photographer on 26th April 1961. No details were recorded. (R.Dyer/Bentley coll.)

105. Fish vans were often attached to passenger trains. On 22nd May 1963, fish was sandwiched between no. 7825 *Lechlade Manor* and the 12.5pm to Paddington. The boxes also contained ice. (P.J.Garland/R.S.Carpenter)

106. The passenger station is beyond the goods shed in this northward view from 12th September 1963. Goods traffic continued into the 1980s, but the sidings were reduced substantially in 1968. (Lens of Sutton coll.)

107. The DMU formed the 14.10 from Swansea on 25th August 1977 and will return there at 17.25. On the right is the outline and fireplace of the building by the signal in picture 106. BR's Sealink operated to Dun Laoghaire briefly in 1978-79. (R.F.Roberts/SLS coll.)

108. A class 101 DMU stands at the shelterless platform on 14th April 1987, by which time the Milford Haven Travel Agency was providing a service for passengers. (B.I.Nathan)

EAST OF MILFORD HAVEN

109. The branch to Gulf's Waterston Refinery came into use on 8th October 1968 and its junction was one mile south of Johnston, at Gulf Branch Junction. There are eight parallel sidings. No. 47473 is leaving in about 1980 with loaded tankers. (N.Sprinks)

WEST OF MILFORD HAVEN

110. The branch to Esso's Herbrandston Refinery came into use on 2nd November 1960 and its junction was two miles south of Johnston, at Herbrandston Junction. A branch west from it at Amoco Junction to Amoco's Robeston Refinery opened on 20th February 1974. We are at the latter on 28th April 1984, approaching some of the eleven parallel sidings. This was the only area to be used in the 21st century for rail transport. (D.H.Mitchell)

Milford Haven	1903	1913	1923	1933
Passenger tickets issued	42138	44900	38543	10593
Season tickets issued	*	*	169	25
Parcels forwarded	422345	585781	730767	935351
General goods forwarded (tons)	1968	3244	3209	2578
Coal and coke received (tons)	82152	103724	80754	229662
Other minerals received (tons)	1603	1652	1763	5213
General goods received (tons)	8849	11156	15613	14889
Coal and Coke handled	4656	23391	126563	22202
Trucks of livestock handled	2	-	87	29

Diagram of the refinery sidings when new. The Herbrandston branch was closed on 10th November 1984. (R.A.Cooke)

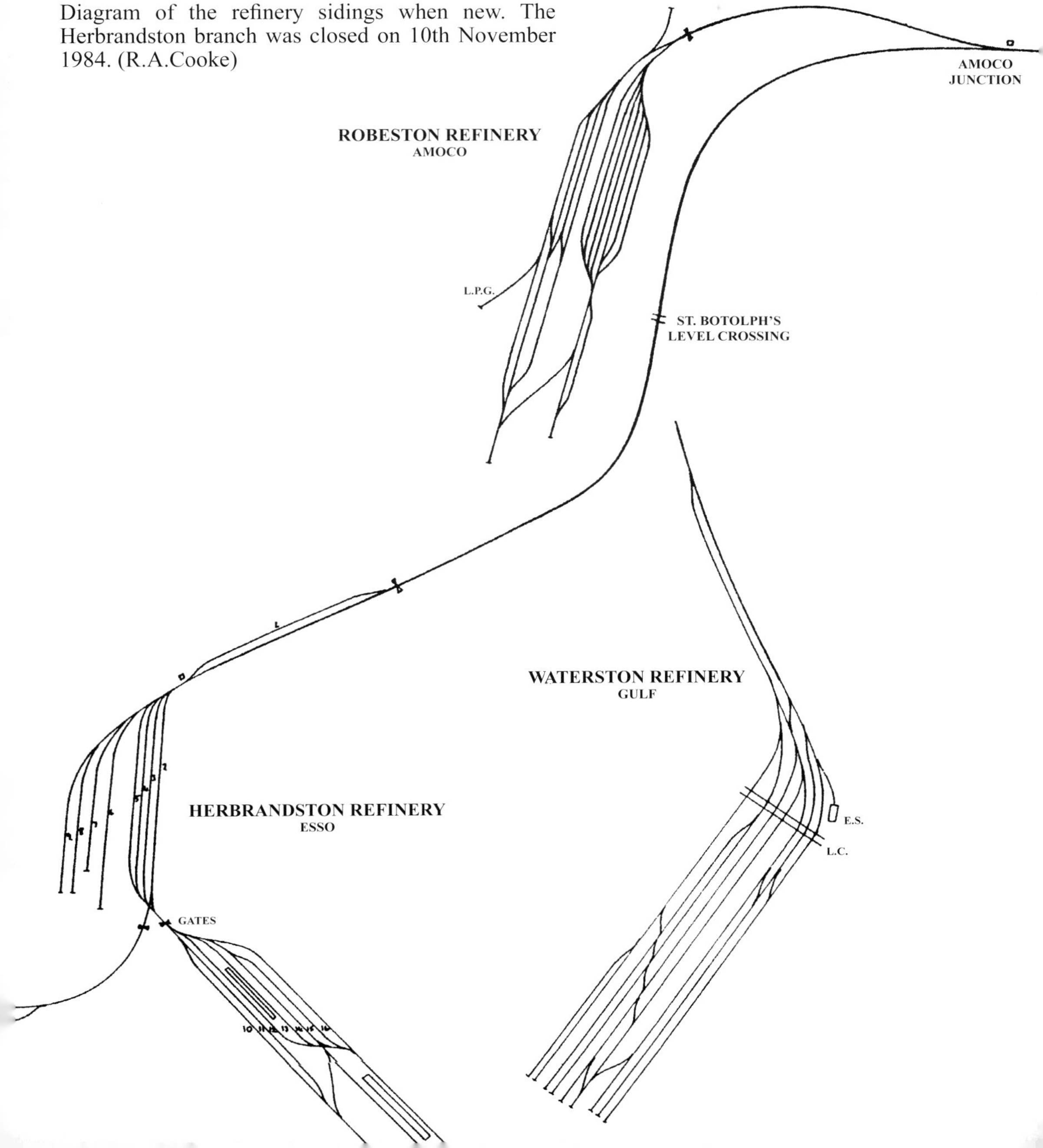

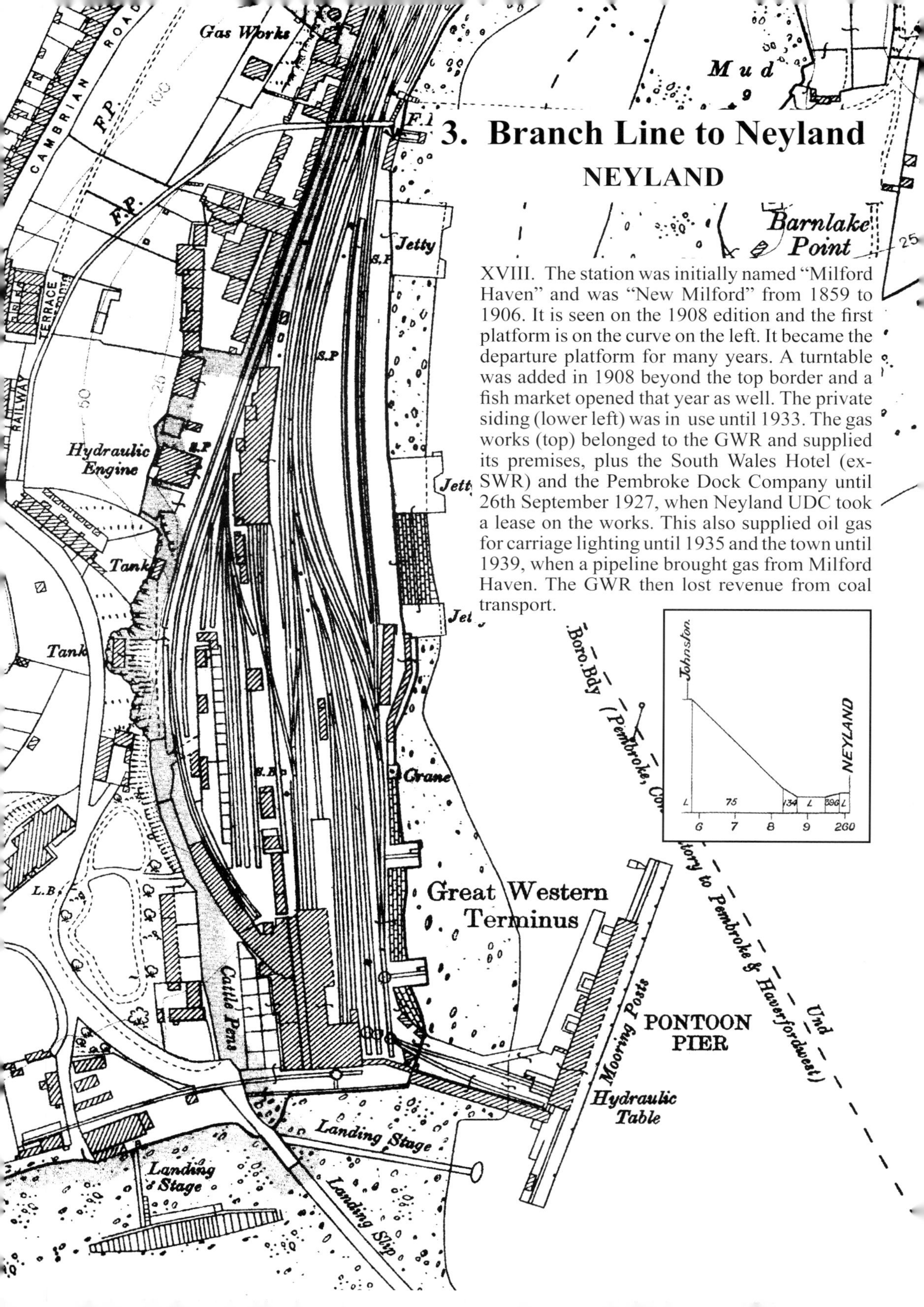

3. Branch Line to Neyland

NEYLAND

XVIII. The station was initially named "Milford Haven" and was "New Milford" from 1859 to 1906. It is seen on the 1908 edition and the first platform is on the curve on the left. It became the departure platform for many years. A turntable was added in 1908 beyond the top border and a fish market opened that year as well. The private siding (lower left) was in use until 1933. The gas works (top) belonged to the GWR and supplied its premises, plus the South Wales Hotel (ex-SWR) and the Pembroke Dock Company until 26th September 1927, when Neyland UDC took a lease on the works. This also supplied oil gas for carriage lighting until 1935 and the town until 1939, when a pipeline brought gas from Milford Haven. The GWR then lost revenue from coal transport.

111. Fish boxes abound in this panorama from sometime before the broad gauge came to an end in 1872. It includes two cattle wagons on the right for imported animals. Nine trawlers were registered here for many years. The first ferry service from here was to Waterford and there were seven ferries based here by 1874. Cork followed, but all was lost to Fishguard in 1906. (A.Dudman coll.)

112. The map shows two groups of cattle pens; access to those in the centre of this picture is across the up running line on the right. The coaches are four-wheeled, putting the photograph at around 1900. There were 63 employed here in 1903, the figure being around 30 in the 1930s. (GWR)

113. A 1921 overview shows that the small pontoons have been greatly extended. Beyond the coaches on the left is the extremely long fish platform. Pembroke is in the background. The coal wagon hoist for bunkering ships is near the end of the quay. (GWR)

XIX. An official diagram from the 1920s includes figures to show the number of four-wheeled wagons which could be put in the sidings. Figures with FT indicate the siding length in feet. It shows both signal boxes (S.B.) (GWR)

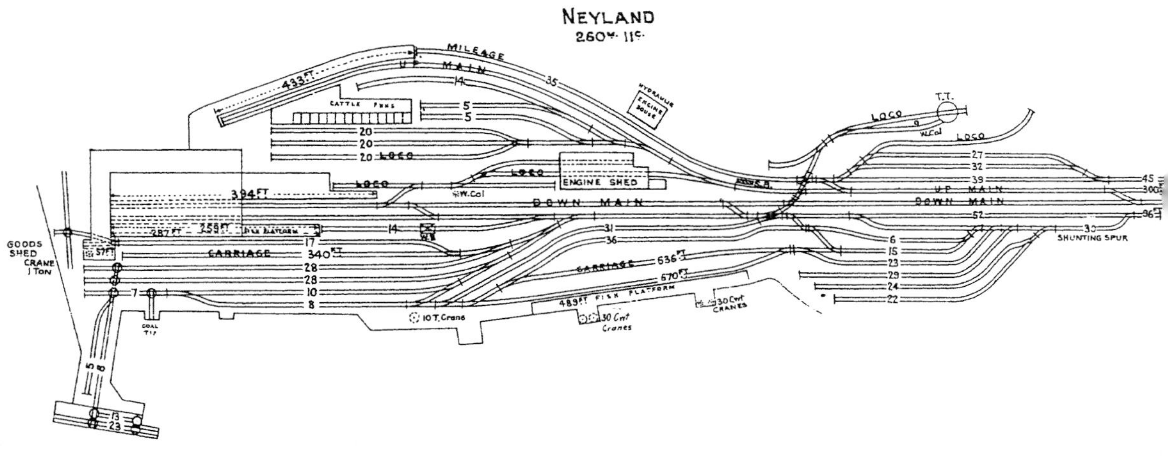

114. Unusually, up trains ran between the engine shed and its turntable, which is on the right of this July 1958 view. The first one was only 40ft and was near the engine shed. The second, a 55ft table, was replaced by one of 65ft at this new site in the 1930s. Included are 0-6-0 no. 2290 and 4-6-0 no. 7829 *Ramsbury Manor*. The tower was part of the hydraulic power system for the cranes and contained its engine and pump. (H.C.Casserley)

115. The simple coaling arrangements were south of the engine shed and are seen on the same day. The view emphasises the cramped nature of the site. (H.C.Casserley)

116. The 7.5am from Johnston has just arrived behind 0-6-0PT no. 3654 on 7th July 1958. The building is probably the original GWR structure of 1863, the year it took over from the SWR. The overall roof had long gone. (H.C.Casserley)

117. Undergoing servicing in the shed in June 1959 were no. 1029 *County of Worcester* and no. 2283, an 0-6-0 of the 2251 class. The engine shed closed on 9th September 1963, when it was coded 87H. It housed 19 locomotives in 1947. (D.K.Jones coll.)

118. No. 1020 *County of Monmouth* and traditional carriage roof boards grace this scene in August 1960. The train has just run into the arrival platform. (D.K.Jones coll.)

Neyland	1903	1913	1923	1933
Passenger tickets issued	52059	40942	41531	17256
Season tickets issued	*	*	291	101
Parcels forwarded	25824	81388	10245	10824
General goods forwarded (tons)	905	1011	613	162
Coal and coke received (tons)	13404	22346	1803	834
Other minerals received (tons)	927	68	229	65
General goods received (tons)	3519	2053	1868	1418
Coal and Coke handled	1421	1946	3294	3029
Trucks of livestock handled	37	25	11	2

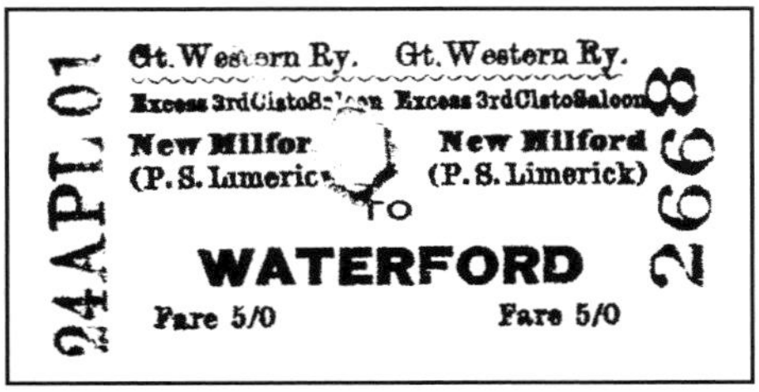

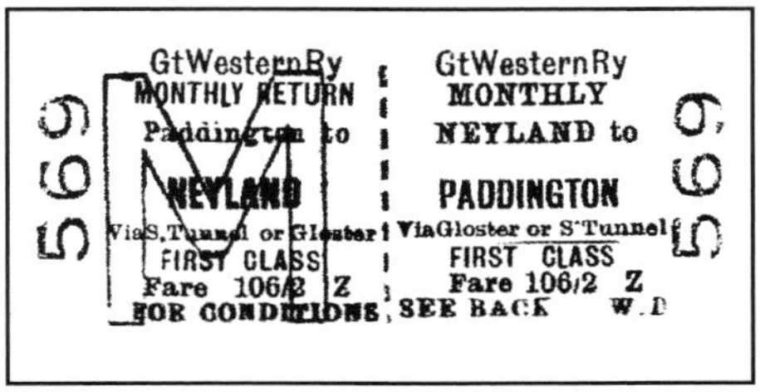

119. The signal box opened in 1919 as Neyland West and lost its suffix on 3rd April 1932, when East closed. The 46-lever frame was in use until 14th June 1964, when the branch closed. These last two pictures are from 20th September 1962. (R.S.Carpenter)

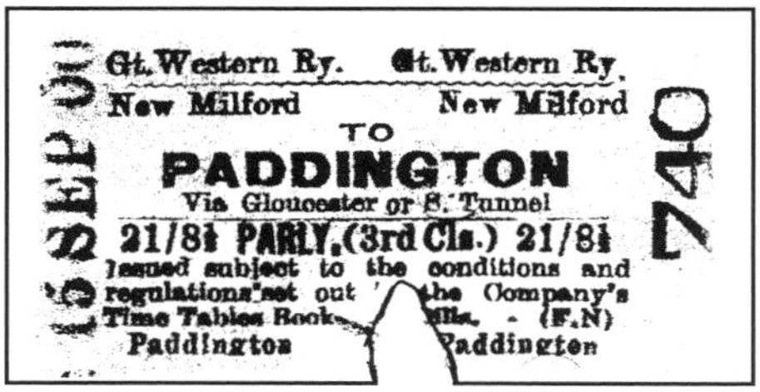

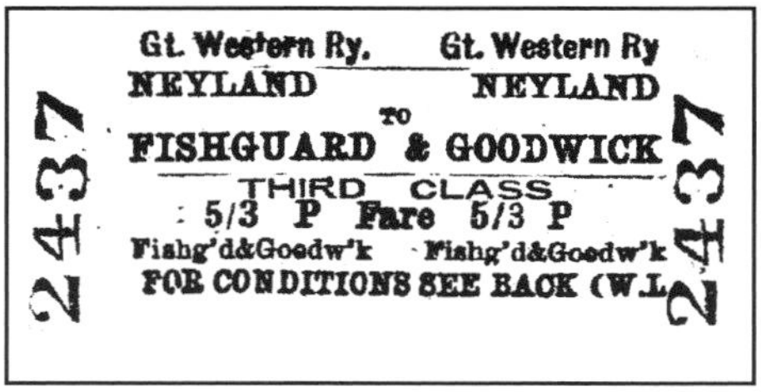

120. Our final view includes one of the many deep water inlets, which made the area so important for commercial and Naval shipping. As its last gasp, the line reopened from 9th May 1966 until 30th September 1968 to meet the demands of the Ministry of Defence, but all has now gone. (R.S.Carpenter)

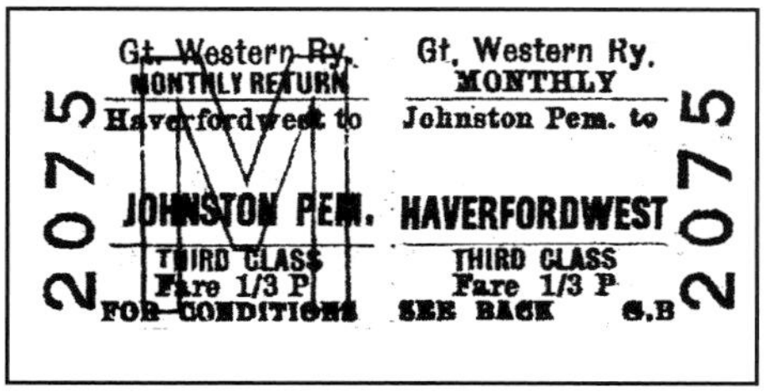

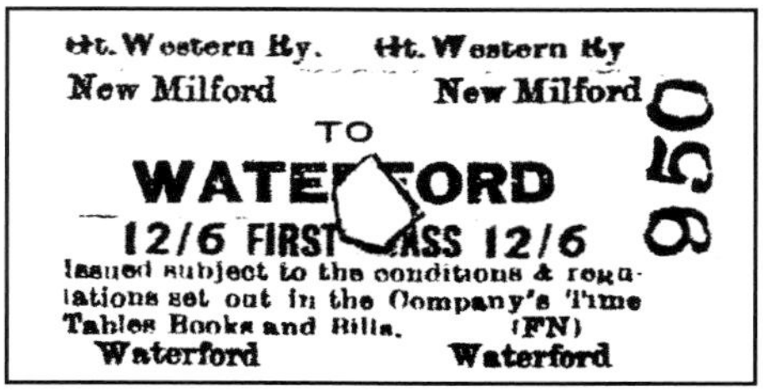

MP Middleton Press

EVOLVING THE ULTIMATE RAIL ENCYCLOPEDIA

Easebourne Lane, Midhurst, West Sussex.
GU29 9AZ Tel:01730 813169

www.middletonpress.co.uk email:info@middletonpress.co.uk
A-978 0 906520 B-978 1 873793 C-978 1 901706 D-978 1 904474 E-978 1 906008

All titles listed below were in print at time of publication - please check current availability by looking at our website - *www.middletonpress.co.uk* or by requesting a Brochure showing our *LATEST* RAILWAY TITLES also our TRAMWAY, TROLLEYBUS, MILITARY and WATERWAYS series

A
Abergavenny to Merthyr C 91 8
Abertillery and Ebbw Vale Lines D 84 5
Allhallows - Branch Line to A 62 8
Alton - Branch Lines to A 11 6
Andover to Southampton A 82 6
Ascot - Branch Lines around A 64 2
Ashburton - Branch Line to B 95 4
Ashford - Steam to Eurostar B 67 1
Ashford to Dover A 48 2
Austrian Narrow Gauge D 04 3
Avonmouth - BL around D 42 5
Aylesbury to Rugby D 91 3

B
Baker Street to Uxbridge D 90 6
Banbury to Birmingham D 27 2
Banbury to Cheltenham E 63 5
Barking to Southend C 80 2
Barmouth to Pwllheli E 53 6
Barry - Branch Lines around D 50 0
Bath Green Park to Bristol C 36 9
Bath to Evercreech Junction A 60 4
Bedford to Wellingborough D 31 9
Birmingham to Wolverhampton E 25 3
Bletchley to Cambridge D 94 4
Bletchley to Rugby E 07 9
Bodmin - Branch Lines around B 83 1
Bournemouth & Poole Trys B 47 3
Bournemouth to Evercreech Jn A 46 8
Bournemouth to Weymouth A 57 4
Brecon to Neath D 43 2
Brecon to Newport D 16 6
Brecon to Newtown E 06 2
Brighton to Eastbourne A 16 1
Brighton to Worthing A 03 1
Bromley South to Rochester B 23 7
Bromsgrove to Birmingham D 87 6
Bromsgrove to Gloucester D 73 9
Brunel - A railtour of his achievements D 74 6
Bude - Branch Line to B 29 9
Burnham to Evercreech Junction B 68 0

C
Cambridge to Ely D 55 5
Canterbury - Branch Lines around B 58 9
Cardiff to Dowlais (Cae Harris) E 47 5
Cardiff to Swansea E 42 0
Carmarthen to Fishguard E 66 6
Caterham & Tattenham Corner B 25 1
Chard and Yeovil - BLs around C 30 7
Charing Cross to Dartford A 75 8
Charing Cross to Orpington A 96 3
Cheddar - Branch Line to B 90 9
Cheltenham to Andover C 43 7
Cheltenham to Redditch D 81 4
Chichester to Portsmouth A 14 7
Clapham Junction to Beckenham Jn B 36 7
Cleobury Mortimer - BLs around E 18 5
Clevedon & Portishead - BLs to D 18 0
Colonel Stephens D 62 3
Consett to South Sheilds E 57 4
Cornwall Narrow Gauge D 56 2
Corris and Vale of Rheidol E 65 9
Craven Arms to Llandeilo E 35 2
Craven Arms to Wellington E 33 8
Crawley to Littlehampton A 34 5
Cromer - Branch Lines around C 26 0
Croydon to East Grinstead B 48 0
Crystal Palace and Catford Loop B 87 1
Cyprus Narrow Gauge E 13 0

D
Darlington - Leamside - Newcastle E 28 4
Darlington to Newcastle D 98 2
Dartford to Sittingbourne B 34 3
Derwent Valley - Branch Line to the D 06 7
Devon Narrow Gauge E 09 3
Didcot to Banbury D 02 9
Didcot to Swindon C 84 0
Didcot to Winchester C 13 0
Dorset & Somerset Narrow Gauge D 76 0
Douglas to Peel C 88 8
Douglas to Port Erin C 55 0
Douglas to Ramsey D 39 5
Dover to Ramsgate A 78 9
Dublin Northwards in the 1950s E 31 4
Dunstable - Branch Lines to E 27 7

E
Ealing to Slough C 42 0
East Cornwall Mineral Railways D 22 7
East Croydon to Three Bridges A 53 6
Eastern Spain Narrow Gauge E 56 7
East Grinstead - Branch Lines to A 07 9
East London - Branch Lines of C 44 4
East London Line B 80 0
Effingham Junction - BLs around A 74 1
Ely to Norwich C 90 1
Enfield Town & Palace Gates - BL to D 32 6
Epsom to Horsham A 30 7
Eritrean Narrow Gauge E 38 3
Euston to Harrow & Wealdstone C 89 5
Exeter to Barnstaple B 15 2
Exeter to Newton Abbot C 49 9
Exeter to Tavistock B 69 5
Exmouth - Branch Lines to B 00 8

F
Fairford - Branch Line to A 52 9
Falmouth, Helston & St. Ives - BL to C 74 1
Fareham to Salisbury A 67 3
Faversham to Dover B 05 3
Felixstowe & Aldeburgh - BL to D 20 3
Fenchurch Street to Barking C 20 8
Festiniog - 50 yrs of enterprise C 83 3
Festiniog 1946-55 E 01 7
Festiniog in the Fifties B 68 8
Festiniog in the Sixties B 91 6
Finsbury Park to Alexandra Palace C 02 8
Frome to Bristol B 77 0

G
Gloucester to Bristol D 35 7
Gloucester to Cardiff D 66 1
Gosport - Branch Lines around A 36 9
Greece Narrow Gauge D 72 2

H
Hampshire Narrow Gauge D 36 4
Harrow to Watford D 14 2
Hastings to Ashford A 37 6
Hawkhurst - Branch Line to A 66 6
Hayling - Branch Line to A 12 3
Hay-on-Wye - Branch Lines around D 92 0
Haywards Heath to Seaford A 28 4
Hemel Hempstead - Branch Lines to D 88 3
Henley, Windsor & Marlow - BL to C77 2
Hereford to Newport D 54 8
Hertford and Hatfield - BLs around E 58 1 6
Hexham to Carlisle D 75 3
Hitchin to Peterborough D 07 4
Holborn Viaduct to Lewisham A 81 9
Horsham - Branch Lines to A 02 4
Huntingdon - Branch Line to A 93 2

I
Ilford to Shenfield C 97 0
Ilfracombe - Branch Line to B 21 3
Industrial Rlys of the South East A 09 3
Ipswich to Saxmundham C 41 3
Isle of Wight Lines - 50 yrs C 12 3

K
Kent Narrow Gauge C 45 1
Kidderminster to Shrewsbury E 10 9
Kingsbridge - Branch Line to C 98 7
Kings Cross to Potters Bar E 62 8
Kingston & Hounslow Loops A 83 3
Kingswear - Branch Line to C 17 8

L
Lambourn - Branch Line to C 70 3
Launceston & Princetown - BL to C 19 2
Lewisham to Dartford A 92 5
Lines around Wimbledon B 75 6
Liverpool Street to Chingford D 01 2
Liverpool Street to Ilford C 34 5
Llandeilo to Swansea E 46 8
London Bridge to Addiscombe B 20 6
London Bridge to East Croydon A 58 1
Longmoor - Branch Lines to A 41 3
Looe - Branch Line to C 22 2
Lowestoft - Branch Lines around E 40 6
Ludlow to Hereford E 14 7
Lydney - Branch Lines around E 26 0
Lyme Regis - Branch Line to A 45 1
Lynton - Branch Line to B 04 6

M
Machynlleth to Barmouth E 54 3
March - Branch Lines around B 09 1
Marylebone to Rickmansworth D 49 4
Melton Constable to Yarmouth Beach E 03 1
Mexborough to Swinton E 36 9
Midhurst - Branch Lines around A 49 9
Mitcham Junction Lines B 01 5
Mitchell & company C 59 8
Monmouth - Branch Lines to E 20 8
Monmouthshire Eastern Valleys D 71 5
Moretonhampstead - BL to C 27 7
Moreton-in-Marsh to Worcester D 26 5
Mountain Ash to Neath D 80 7

N
Newbury to Westbury C 66 6
Newcastle to Hexham D 69 2
Newport (IOW) - Branch Lines to A 26 0
Newquay - Branch Lines to C 71 0
Newton Abbot to Plymouth C 60 4
Newtown to Aberystwyth E 41 3
North East German Narrow Gauge D 44 9
Northern France Narrow Gauge C 75 8
North London Line B 94 7
North Woolwich - BLs around C 65 9

O
Ongar - Branch Line to E 05 5
Oswestry - Branch Lines around E 60 4
Oxford to Bletchley D 57 9
Oxford to Moreton-in-Marsh D 15 9

P
Paddington to Ealing C 37 6
Paddington to Princes Risborough C 81 9
Padstow - Branch Line to B 54 1
Peterborough to Kings Lynn E 32 1
Plymouth - BLs around B 98 5
Plymouth to St. Austell C 63 5
Pontypool to Mountain Ash D 65 4
Porthmadog 1954-94 - BL around B 31 2
Portmadoc 1923-46 - BL around B 13 8
Portsmouth to Southampton A 31 4
Portugal Narrow Gauge E 67 3
Potters Bar to Cambridge D 70 8
Princes Risborough - Branch Lines to D 05 0
Princes Risborough to Banbury C 85 7

R
Reading to Basingstoke B 27 5
Reading to Didcot C 79 6
Reading to Guildford A 47 5
Redhill to Ashford A 73 4
Return to Blaenau 1970-82 C 64 2
Rhymney and New Tredegar Lines E 48 2
Rickmansworth to Aylesbury D 61 6
Romania & Bulgaria Narrow Gauge E 23 9
Romneyrail C 32 1
Ross-on-Wye - Branch Lines around E 30 7
Rugby to Birmingham E 37 6
Ryde to Ventnor A 19 2

S
Salisbury to Westbury B 39 8
Saxmundham to Yarmouth C 69 7
Saxony Narrow Gauge D 47 0
Seaton & Sidmouth - Branch Lines to A 95 6
Selsey - Branch Line to A 04 8
Sheerness - Branch Line to B 16 2
Shrewsbury - Branch Line to A 86 4
Shrewsbury to Ludlow E 21 5
Shrewsbury to Newtown E 29 1
Sierra Leone Narrow Gauge D 28 9
Sirhowy Valley Line E 12 3
Sittingbourne to Ramsgate A 90 1
Slough to Newbury C 56 7
South African Two-foot gauge E 51 2
Southampton to Bournemouth A 42
Southern France Narrow Gauge C 47
South London Line B 46 6
Southwold - Branch Line to A 15 4
Spalding - Branch Lines around E 52
St Albans to Bedford D 08 1
St. Austell to Penzance C 67 3
Steaming through the Isle of Wight A
Steaming through West Hants A 69
Stourbridge to Wolverhampton E 16
St. Pancras to Barking D 68 5
St. Pancras to St. Albans C 78 9
Stratford-upon-Avon to Birmingham
Stratford-upon-Avon to Cheltenham
Surrey Narrow Gauge C 87 1
Sussex Narrow Gauge C 68 0
Swanley to Ashford B 45 9
Swansea to Carmarthen E 59 8
Swindon to Bristol C 96 3
Swindon to Gloucester D 46 3
Swindon to Newport D 30 2
Swiss Narrow Gauge C 94 9

T
Talyllyn - 50 years C 39 0
Taunton to Barnstaple B 60 2
Taunton to Exeter C 82 6
Tavistock to Plymouth B 88 6
Tenterden - Branch Line to A 21 5
Three Bridges to Brighton A 35 2
Tilbury Loop C 86 4
Tiverton - Branch Lines around C 62
Tivetshall to Beccles D 41 8
Tonbridge to Hastings A 44 4
Torrington - Branch Lines to B 37 4
Towcester - Branch Lines around E 3
Tunbridge Wells - Branch Lines to A

U
Upwell - Branch Line to B 64 0

V
Victoria to Bromley South A 98 7
Vivarais Revisited E 08 6

W
Wantage - Branch Line to D 25 8
Wareham to Swanage - 50 yrs D 09
Waterloo to Windsor A 54 3
Waterloo to Woking A 38 3
Watford to Leighton Buzzard D 45 6
Welshpool to Llanfair E 49 9
Wenford Bridge to Fowey C 09 3
Westbury to Bath B 55 8
Westbury to Taunton C 76 5
West Cornwall Mineral Railways D 4
West Croydon to Epsom B 08 4
West German Narrow Gauge D 93 7
West London - Branch Lines of C 50
West London Line B 84 8
West Wiltshire - Branch Lines of D 1
Weymouth - Branch Lines around A
Willesden Junction to Richmond B 7
Wimbledon to Beckenham C 58 1
Wimbledon to Epsom B 62 6
Wimborne - Branch Lines around A
Wisbech 1800-1901 C 93 2
Wisbech - Branch Lines around C 0
Woking to Alton A 59 8
Woking to Portsmouth A 25 3
Woking to Southampton A 55 0
Wolverhampton to Shrewsbury E 44
Worcester to Birmingham D 97 5
Worcester to Hereford D 38 8
Worthing to Chichester A 06 2

Y
Yeovil - 50 yrs change C 38 3
Yeovil to Dorchester A 76 5
Yeovil to Exeter A 91 8